SPINNING INTO BUTTER

A Play in Two Acts
by
REBECCA GILMAN

Dramatic Publishing
Woodstock, Illinois • England • Australia • New Zealand

IMPORTANT BILLING AND CREDIT REQUIREMENTS

All producers of SPINNING INTO BUTTER *must* give credit to the author(s) of the play in all programs distributed in connection with performances of the play and in all instances in which the title of the play appears for purposes of advertising, publicizing or otherwise exploiting the play and/or a production. The name of the author(s) *must* also appear on a separate line, on which no other name appears, immediately following the title, and *must* appear in size of type not less than fifty percent the size of the title type. Biographical information on the author(s), if included in this book, may be used on all programs.

All producers of the Play must include the following acknowledgment on the title page of all programs distributed in connection with performances of the Play and on all advertising and promotional materials:

"Originally produced by the Goodman Theatre, Chicago, Illinois, on February 22, 1999, Robert Falls, Artistic Director, Roche Schulfer, Executive Director." "Produced by Lincoln Center Theatre in 2000, New York City."

On all programs this notices must appear:

"Produced by special arrangement with
THE DRAMATIC PUBLISHING COMPANY of Woodstock, Illinois"

SPINNING INTO BUTTER

A Play in Two Acts
For 5 Men and 2 Women

CHARACTERS

SARAH DANIELS. . . . . 35-40, dean of students
ROSS COLLINS. . . . . 35-40, an Art History professor
DEAN CATHERINE KENNEY 60
DEAN BURTON STRAUSS . . 55, chair of Humanities Dept.
MR. MEYERS . . . . 50, a security guard
PATRICK CHIBAS . . . . 19, a self-assured young man
GREG SULLIVAN. . . . . 21, a senior

TIME and PLACE
Belmont College, Belmont, Vermont, in the present.

Approximate running time: 2 hours and 15 minutes
Set requirements: Single set

ACT ONE

SCENE ONE

SETTING: *A dean's office at Belmont College, a small liberal arts college in Belmont, Vermont. It is a large office, with built-in bookshelves full of books, nice white trimming and a large warm rug on the floor. The desk is large and cluttered with papers and more books and there are several, very comfortable-looking chairs. There may even be a fireplace. Large windows allow a lot of light.*

AT RISE: *At the desk is SARAH DANIELS who is the college's dean of students. She is earnest in her desire to do right by her students. There is a knock at the door.*

SARAH. Come in.

> *(PATRICK CHIBAS enters. He is nineteen, self-assured, dressed in running shorts and a T-shirt.)*

PATRICK. Dean Daniels? I think I was next. I got a note in my box that said you wanted to see me?
SARAH *(smiles)*. I left notes for a lot of students. *(He stares at her.)* I need you to tell me your name.
PATRICK. Oh. Sorry. Patrick Chibas.
SARAH. Patrick. Great. Have a seat. *(He takes a seat and looks around while she fishes a file out from a pile on*

her desk. While she looks:) Welcome back. How's moving going?

PATRICK. Fine.

SARAH *(finds his file but doesn't open it yet).* What dorm are you in this year?

PATRICK. Grange Hall.

SARAH. Was that your first choice?

PATRICK. Last.

SARAH. I guess sophomores always get the short straw, don't they?

PATRICK. Yeah.

SARAH. Did you go home for the summer?

PATRICK. For the first part and then I went to Florida.

SARAH. Did you have an internship?

PATRICK. No. I just bummed around. I waited tables at the Fish Shack.

SARAH. Just relaxed, huh?

PATRICK. Yeah. *(Small beat.)* Am I in trouble?

SARAH. No! No. I'm sorry, Patrick. I actually wanted to talk to you about a scholarship. *(Opening his file.)*

PATRICK. Oh yeah?

SARAH. Yeah. You declared an environmental sciences major last spring.

PATRICK. Yeah.

SARAH. Well, we have a scholarship that's designated for...well, it's designated for an outstanding minority student in environmental sciences, and I just wondered if you might be interested.

PATRICK. Sure.

SARAH. Good. There's just one thing, then. I need to ask you, Patrick, on your Belmont application, you...under the voluntary disclosure of your racial/ethnic background you marked "other."

PATRICK. Yeah.

SARAH. Okay. I guess I need to know, so I can make a recommendation to the board, just what "other" is. If you don't mind.

PATRICK. I don't mind. I'm Nuyorican.

SARAH. Nuyorican?

PATRICK. Yeah.

SARAH. Huh. Would it be fair for me to say, then, that you're, um, Hispanic?

PATRICK. I prefer Nuyorican.

SARAH. Of course. I just... well, to simplify things, when I make my recommendation to the board, do you think I could just mention that you're Hispanic?

PATRICK. What's wrong with Nuyorican?

SARAH. Nothing, of course.

PATRICK. Then why don't you just say that?

SARAH. I will. *(Beat.)* And then, I think, I'll probably be asked to explain and I wondered, could I just explain by saying that you're Hispanic?

PATRICK. Why would you be asked to explain?

SARAH. Because the members of our scholarship advisory board are... well... to be honest, Patrick, they're not culturally sensitive. *(He stares at her.)* If you know what I mean.

PATRICK. I guess I don't.

SARAH. I think they tend to see the world in very... limited terms, as black or white or re... *(She stops herself.)* ... racially divided along solid, clearly delineated lines.

PATRICK. So you're saying they're old?

SARAH. Yes. They're old. And they're just...they're not going to know what Nuyorican is.

PATRICK *(sighs)*. Look, you understand why I don't want to be called Hispanic, don't you?

SARAH. As I understand it, and correct me, please, if I'm wrong, it's because it really only applies to imperialists of European descent who colonized Puerto Rico.

PATRICK. Yeah. I mean, if you understand, then...

SARAH. Why am I suggesting it. Good question. *(Beat.)* And you're right. I shouldn't compromise your feelings for the sake of expediency. I'm sorry.

PATRICK. That's okay.

SARAH *(thinking)*. What about Latino?

PATRICK *(irritated)*. No.

SARAH. How 'bout just plain Puerto Rican?

PATRICK. No.

SARAH *(beat)*. It's a twelve-thousand-dollar scholarship, Patrick.

PATRICK. It is?

SARAH. I want you to get it. It just seems like a shame to me to leave money sitting around in a bank when it could be doing you some good. You're a remarkably talented student and I think you should be rewarded in a meaningful way. *(Long pause.)*

PATRICK. You can put Puerto Rican.

SARAH *(smiles)*. Thank you. *(She makes a note.)* I'll let you know as soon as I hear.

PATRICK. This is a lot better than I expected. I thought I was in trouble.

SARAH. Far from it.

PATRICK. Great. Thanks a lot, Dean Daniels.

SARAH. You're welcome. Will you send in whoever's next?

PATRICK. Sure.

(*PATRICK opens the office door. As he does, ROSS COLLINS enters. He is an Art History professor in his late thirties. He is handsome and energetic.*)

ROSS (*to SARAH*). Hey. (*To PATRICK.*) Hi there.

PATRICK. Hi, Dr. Collins. (*He exits. ROSS closes the door.*)

ROSS. Is he one of my students?

SARAH. I don't know.

ROSS. Have you got a second?

SARAH. I don't know, Ross. There are a ton of kids out there.

ROSS. Just a second?

SARAH. Okay. (*He doesn't say anything.*) So where were you last night?

ROSS. God, it was a nightmare. Petra's plane was five hours late and we didn't leave the city until midnight. We just got back.

SARAH. It took you ... ten hours?

ROSS. We stopped in Lake George and got a room at a motel. Petra couldn't drive and I kept nodding off, so we stopped and I got some sleep. We drove the rest of the way this morning.

SARAH. Oh.

ROSS. Are you angry?

SARAH. You said you'd come by. When you got in.

ROSS. I'm sorry. I should have called.

SARAH. Well, it's not like it was prom night.

ROSS (*laughs*). Prom night. (*Beat.*)

SARAH. So how is Petra?

ROSS. She's fine, I guess. We didn't have much of a chance to talk. She fell asleep as soon as we hit the road.

SARAH. That's why she couldn't drive?

ROSS. She doesn't know how. She doesn't have a license.

SARAH. Oh.

ROSS. She grew up in Manhattan.

SARAH. Right. *(Beat.)* So how was her sabbatical?

ROSS. Amazing apparently. She spent a few months traveling, watching dance, and then she worked with a troop in Braunschweig who were all refugees from Bosnia. They developed an adaptation of *The Cherry Orchard.* Can you imagine? This Russian classic? These refugees from a collapsed communist state?

SARAH. Were they Muslims or Serbs?

ROSS. I don't know. Is it important?

SARAH. No, it's just, if they were Muslims...and then, Chekov and communism...

ROSS. And?

SARAH. I don't know. I don't get it.

ROSS. You don't?

SARAH. It seems arbitrary.

ROSS. Maybe you had to be there.

SARAH. Petra did the thing where everybody in the audience had to take off their shoes, right?

ROSS. The piece on the World Bank. Right.

SARAH. I didn't get that either.

ROSS. I probably didn't do it justice. *(Beat.)*

SARAH. So do you want to do something tonight?

ROSS. I don't know. *(Small beat. Racking his brain.)* Oh, God! I can't believe I almost forgot to tell you this! This is precisely what I wanted to tell you because I knew you'd appreciate it! Okay. I got into the city at eleven or so, and I parked the car at a garage, then I decided to go to MOMA after all to see that Cambodian exhibit.

SARAH. I thought you said it wasn't art.

ROSS. It wasn't, but I wanted to see it anyway. But before I get to that, I got on the subway and at the next stop this man gets on and sits next to me ... *(Gesturing.)* ... and I think to myself, "I've seen this man before." And while I'm trying to place him he reaches in his coat pocket and he pulls out this small, laminated card and he holds it right in front of his face and he's studying it, furiously. So I glanced over to see what he was reading and it's a Bible verse. You know? Like "John 12:24." And so I take another look at him. And that's when I notice that, while he's very neatly dressed, his clothes are rather shabby. His suit, for example, is too small and his shirt cuffs are fully exposed and they're stained at the edges and the hem of his trousers is frayed and his shoes are showing cracks in the leather. And then it hits me! The last time I was on a train in Manhattan I saw this very same man. Wearing this very same suit and reading this very same card to himself. I've been on the subway precisely four times in the past year—not since last Christmas—and twice, consecutively, I've seen this very same man. *(Beat.)* Now what are the chances of that?

SARAH. Small?

ROSS. I felt both times that he was a man about to disintegrate. A man who kept himself in one piece by a dedicated devotion to God. But a devotion that was so fragile that he literally had to keep it here, before his face, like a beacon. *(Pause.)*

SARAH. That's precisely what you wanted to tell me?

ROSS. I wanted to tell you that. Yes.

SARAH. Did you sleep with Petra?

ROSS. Last night?

SARAH. Yes.

ROSS. No. I didn't sleep with Petra last night.

SARAH. Good, then. So do you want to do something to-night?

ROSS. That's the other thing I wanted to tell you. (*Beat. SARAH waits.*) I really... I'm really sorry but I can't keep seeing you.

SARAH. What?

ROSS (*rehearsed*). I think it's for the best. We agreed up front that we weren't working toward a permanent relationship and I think now's the time to make a break. It's a natural breaking point.

SARAH. Why?

ROSS. Well, the thing is this: Petra is back from her sabbatical. And what I haven't told you, is that before Petra left for her sabbatical, we were involved.

SARAH. You were *what*?

ROSS. We've been lovers for several years.

SARAH. Lovers?

ROSS. Or partners. Whatever you want to say.

SARAH. And did you break up or... ?

ROSS. No, we just sort of took a break. I mean, Petra was going away and we didn't know what the year would hold. So we agreed we could see other people while we were apart.

SARAH. So does Petra know about me?

ROSS. I told her a while ago.

SARAH. Then could you have had the decency to tell *me* about *her*?!

ROSS. I kept meaning to, but...there never seemed to be a good time.

SARAH. That's the dumbest thing I ever heard!

ROSS. Please don't be angry.

SARAH. So what was I, then? A temp?

ROSS. No, Sarah. Don't belittle yourself. You're a wonderful woman. You know that. Smart and funny and attractive.

SARAH. Fuck that.

ROSS. Please.

SARAH. No, I mean it. Fuck that. You don't mean that. You don't mean that about me.

ROSS. Sarah—

SARAH. This is so embarrassing. Everybody must know about you and Petra.

ROSS. I don't know. Our friends do. The faculty. *(Beat.)* Some students.

SARAH. And nobody had the decency to tell me?

ROSS. That's the second time you've used that word, "decency."

SARAH. Decency is hardly a lot to expect.

ROSS. Look, I know I should have told you, but I couldn't bring myself to do it. You were so vulnerable.

SARAH. Vulnerable?

ROSS. You said yourself how lonely you were when you moved to Vermont, how much my company meant to you.

SARAH. I did not say that. I said I could not relate to anybody on the faculty because everybody had a stupid name like "Petra" and nobody knew how to do anything practical like drive a car.

ROSS. There's no reason to say cruel things about someone you've never met.

SARAH. Okay, I apologize. Now you apologize to me for lying.

ROSS. I didn't lie.

SARAH. You did not tell me the whole truth. You equivocated and equivocation is the same as lying.

ROSS. That's your fundamentalist background talking.

SARAH. No no no. That's Merriam-Webster talking. *(She picks up a dictionary and starts flipping pages.)*

ROSS. I don't need you to define the term for me.

SARAH *(reading)*. "Equivocal."

ROSS. I'm not an idiot.

SARAH. "Subject to two or more interpretations and usually used to mislead or confuse." That's what you did. You misled me.

ROSS. This wrangling over the particulars is not going to change the big picture. As I said, you're a smart, funny and attractive woman and I hope, sincerely, that we can now be friends.

SARAH. Please.

ROSS. Look, we're going to run into each other all the time. We have a committee meeting on Monday. *(Beat. SARAH doesn't answer.)* Sarah. *(Beat.)* I'm really sorry. It probably doesn't sound like I am because I'm really ... I'm not very good at these things. I even practiced what I was going to say.

SARAH. I could tell.

ROSS. Because I'm not very good at it. I never in my life thought I'd have two girlfriends.

SARAH. Girlfriends?

ROSS. Partners. Whatever. I never really dated until graduate school. I had bad skin. It made me shy.

SARAH. Well you don't have bad skin now.

ROSS. I know! I... *(Realizing he's too enthusiastic.)* It's just, it's been flattering. The fact that women are actually interested in me.

SARAH. Small pond.

ROSS *(beat. He swallows it)*. Well, at any rate, what I want to get across is that I really am sorry.

SARAH *(beat)*. It's okay. It's just that I don't have any friends here. That's all.

ROSS. I'm sorry.

SARAH. Forget it. It doesn't matter. You want to be friends?

ROSS. I really do.

SARAH. Fine. We're friends.

ROSS. Great. *(He pulls her into a hug which she tolerates, releases her.)* Well. You've got a hundred students waiting to see you.

SARAH. Yes, I do.

ROSS *(at the door)*. Do you want to have lunch one day this week? Wednesday?

SARAH. Why don't you call me.

ROSS. Okay.

SARAH. Okay. *(He opens the door and exits. SARAH crosses to the open door and makes a motion to a student we can't see.)* Hold on. I just need to make a phone call. *(She closes the door behind her.)* Christ. *(She stands for a moment. The chimes on the chapel next door sound their tune, then begin to count out the hour. It is ten o'clock. Somewhere in the middle, SARAH gathers herself and turns back and opens her office door.)* Okay. Next?

BLACKOUT

SCENE TWO

A week later. Sarah's office. Dean CATHERINE KEN-NEY, BURTON STRAUSS, chair of the Humanities De-partment, and ROSS are in the middle of a heated argu-ment.

ROSS. But they're supposed to design their own major. That's why it's called Independent Studies.

STRAUSS. I'm not trying to change that. I'm just saying that we should draw up a list and make them choose from the list. Otherwise they'll just take a bunch of crap and graduate.

KENNEY. We don't offer any "crap."

STRAUSS. What about those winter term classes? How fast did "Wine Tasting" fill up last year?

KENNEY. Wine tasting is a valuable skill.

STRAUSS. Or "The Films of Brigitte Bardot"? Or "Art Appreciation"?

ROSS. I teach that.

KENNEY. Winter term is an exception.

STRAUSS. Why?

KENNEY. Because. It's only one month. In the winter.

STRAUSS. But why should they waste it?

KENNEY. Because. *(Beat.)* That's when they ski. All right?

STRAUSS. What?

KENNEY. Sixty-seven percent of students surveyed said that the ski slope was a deciding factor in choosing Bel-mont over competing colleges.

STRAUSS. I should have known.

ROSS. Okay. Should we vote on the courses?

KENNEY. We don't have a quorum without Sarah.

STRAUSS. Do we have to wait for her?

KENNEY. Yes.

STRAUSS. Why is she even on the committee? She doesn't know anything about pedagogy.

KENNEY. She knows enough.

STRAUSS. Don't I get some votes by proxy?

KENNEY. Why should you?

STRAUSS. As chair?

KENNEY. No. We'll have to wait. *(Long pause. She looks around.)* Does her office seem bigger than mine?

STRAUSS. No.

KENNEY. I think it's bigger.

STRAUSS. I don't think it is.

KENNEY. I'm going to walk it off. *(She crosses to a wall and begins walking the distance, counting the steps on her fingers.)* One ... two ... three ...

STRAUSS. There's just less stuff in it.

KENNEY. You can't tell with these colonial buildings. Everything's irregular.

STRAUSS. They were master craftsmen.

KENNEY. They were drunks. Put a marble on that floor and it will roll straight to the corner.

STRAUSS. It's an old building. It's settled.

KENNEY. Do it.

ROSS. Please. Could we at least discuss scheduling for the spring? Something pertinent.

KENNEY *(finishes walking the length of the wall)*. Oh fine! It's not bigger at all. It's smaller.

STRAUSS. See.

KENNEY. See what?

(SARAH enters, hurriedly.)

KENNEY. You're late.

SARAH. There's a problem. Someone's been leaving threatening, racist notes on the door of one of our African American students.

KENNEY. Please tell me you're kidding.

ROSS *(overlapping).* Oh my God.

SARAH. You should look at them. *(She holds out two notes. They gather around and read, passing them amongst themselves. As they read.)* He said he was willing to ignore the first one but then he found this one this afternoon and it was so ... graphic. *(Pause. They read, silenced. Then ...)*

ROSS. God.

KENNEY. And you say somebody just left this on his door?

SARAH. Yes. When he got the second one he took them over to security and they called me.

KENNEY. Which dorm is he in?

SARAH. Houghton Hall. He's a freshman.

KENNEY. I've never seen anything like this before.

SARAH. His name is Simon Brick.

ROSS. Is he all right? Is he frightened?

SARAH. I don't know. I haven't talked to him yet. He left the notes and went on to class.

KENNEY. Do you think we should call him over? I could send somebody to his class ...

SARAH. I left a message asking him to come see me when he gets in. If he wanted to go to class I thought we should let him. Whatever's easiest for him is what I was thinking. *(Beat.)* He doesn't even have a roommate.

KENNEY. He has a single?

SARAH. There are those two in Houghton.

KENNEY. I thought they were reserved for sophomores.

SARAH. We can't get sophomores to live in a freshman dorm.

STRAUSS *(who's been studying the notes)*. Rooming accommodations? Is this what you want to talk about?

SARAH. I just thought you would want to know something about him.

STRAUSS. Yes, yes, but first we have to decide.

KENNEY. Decide what?

STRAUSS *(indicating the notes)*. What do we do? How do we punish this racist?

SARAH. Won't we expel him?

ROSS. Or her.

STRAUSS *(overlapping)*. That's a defensive action. We have to be pro-active on this. We must make it known, loud and clear, that this sentiment is not Belmont. That Belmont cannot be reduced to this trash. We should issue some sort of statement, right away, condemning this—

SARAH *(interrupting)*. I think we should try to find out who did it.

KENNEY. Technically I should call President Garvey and ask him what to do.

ROSS. Garvey won't know what to do. He's so out of touch. Burton's right. I think we should make a public gesture of some sort. We should call an all-campus meeting so we can discuss what's going on.

STRAUSS. Yes.

SARAH. Don't you think we should talk to Simon first?

ROSS. Look, we pride ourselves on our inclusiveness. We claim to embrace cultural diversity. And yet some racist is running loose on campus, and I would wager that this idiot is very much like all our other students in appearance and manner and class, and that's what we need to reveal. That racism isn't somebody else's problem. It's our problem. If we handle this right, it could be a real learning experience for the students.

STRAUSS. Exactly.

KENNEY. All right then. Good. This seems like the sort of response we should have, doesn't it? In case any of the parents call I can tell them we've organized this meeting and everything is under control. That's usually all they want to know.

SARAH. I thought you'd never seen anything like this before.

KENNEY. Not like this, no. So, shall I propose this campus forum thingee to President Garvey? I'll tell him everyone at the committee meeting thinks it's a good idea. He doesn't have to know that we're missing half the people.

ROSS. I strongly recommend it. You can tell him that.

STRAUSS. As do I.

SARAH. We're moving too fast. We should talk to Simon, first. What if he doesn't want us to talk about him this way?

STRAUSS. Why wouldn't he?

SARAH. I just think it might be embarrassing for him. *(They don't get it.)* He's very quiet. Everyone would stare.

STRAUSS. No one will stare.

KENNEY. All right then. We should put out a memo to the faculty before we call the students together. Ross?

ROSS. I'll be glad to write something up. Burton?

STRAUSS. I'll be glad to help. *(A knock on the door.)*

KENNEY & SARAH. Come in.

(MR. MEYERS, a security guard enters, carrying a plastic bag.)

MEYERS. Oh. Excuse me.

SARAH. It's all right, Mr. Meyers. What is it?

MEYERS. The police said we should put the notes in this bag to protect the fingerprints.

KENNEY. The police! You didn't call the police, Sarah?

SARAH. Yes.

KENNEY. Never do that!

SARAH. I—

KENNEY. It'll be in the local press and then the wire services pick it up and then we're everybody's business! Really! How could you be so stupid?

SARAH. I thought since the note was so violent—

KENNEY. It's an internal incident. Internal. You've seriously overstepped your bounds here, Sarah.

SARAH. I thought I was fully authorized—

KENNEY (*overlapping*). I'm not going to quibble with you. I've *got* to call Garvey now.

MEYERS. The police are waiting for you in your office. They wanted to talk to somebody in charge.

KENNEY. And you thought that was me, did you? (*She exits and he follows.*)

STRAUSS. I was wondering who we should get to lead the forum.

ROSS. I'd like to put my own name in.

STRAUSS. As would I, of course.

SARAH. I still think we should wait.

STRAUSS. But you didn't say anything to convince us, did you. You're not going to persuade until you learn to argue effectively. But they don't teach you social workers how to argue, they only teach you how to console.

SARAH. I'm not a social worker.

STRAUSS. Ayn Rand was right about your lot. *(He laughs.)* Come down to my office, Ross, and let's draft that memo.

ROSS. I'll be right there. *(He exits. ROSS looks at SARAH and closes the door behind STRAUSS.)* You did the right thing, calling the police.

SARAH. No shit. *(Small beat.)* I mean, thanks.

ROSS. Look, I know you don't agree with me about the forum, but it's such a small campus, and rumors will start. It's probably better for Simon if we discuss it openly, so people will know exactly what's going on.

SARAH. I think it's better for Simon if we respect his privacy.

ROSS. So you don't think the personal is political?

SARAH. I think the personal is personal. Speaking of which, I'm getting lots of sympathetic stares lately, so I'm assuming the word is out that you and Petra are back together.

ROSS. I guess it is. I was actually hoping we could avoid all this junior-high stuff and you two could just meet each other. We're hosting a salon Saturday night, if you'd like to come.

SARAH. A salon?

ROSS. Yeah, we started them a couple of years ago. People read what they've been working on, or bring some art work. Would you like to come?

SARAH. Boy. You know? I'd rather have my eyeballs gouged out with soup spoons.

ROSS *(smiles)*. Well, then. *(Beat.)* How violent your opinions are when they don't matter.

SARAH. Wait a minute. You and Petra live together?

ROSS. Yes.

SARAH. In your house?

ROSS. Yes.

SARAH. Where were her things?

ROSS. You're still mad at me, aren't you?

SARAH. Her little ballet shoes. Her tutus?

ROSS. She doesn't wear tutus.

SARAH *(grabs a book from the shelf and shoves it at him).* Take this book you gave me. Take it back.

ROSS *(takes it, looks).* The Rilke? Sarah. You have to keep the Rilke. This book changed my life. *(Puts it back on her desk.)* Look, why don't we talk later? After things have settled down. *(SARAH doesn't answer.)* Just ... read the Rilke.

(He leaves. Immediately, SARAH takes up the Rilke and throws it at the door. A loud thud.)

MEYERS *(off).* Hello?

SARAH. Hello?

(MR. MEYERS cracks the door.)

MEYERS. Hello?

SARAH. Hi.

MEYERS. The police took the notes.

SARAH. What'd they say?

MEYERS. They think it was a student. Nobody from town would really know there was a black kid in that particular room.

SARAH. That makes sense I guess.

MEYERS. They said they'd take fingerprints off them.

SARAH. We all touched them.

MEYERS. Yeah. They said they'd maybe ask for some handwriting samples. Just for comparison.

SARAH. Whose?

MEYERS. Other students in the dorm, prob'ly.

SARAH. This is awful.

MEYERS. I know. *(Picks up the Rilke.)* You dropped your book.

SARAH. I threw my book.

MEYERS. You don't like it?

SARAH. Actually, no, I've always hated Rilke.

MEYERS *(nods).* It's sort of small. I find I feel better if I throw heavy things. Maybe a dictionary. Or a thesaurus. *(SARAH laughs.)* Here. *(He hands her the book.)* I've worked here twenty years, Sarah, and one thing I've learned, these people don't know their ass from a hole in the ground. *(SARAH laughs again.)* After twenty years, you find it's not so funny. *(SARAH stops laughing.)*

BLACKOUT

SCENE THREE

Two weeks later. SARAH is talking to GREG SULLIVAN, a senior. GREG is very much the Belmont man. He is handsome, self-assured, well-educated.

GREG. I guess when we heard about the thing with the notes, it was almost so horrific that it made us numb. Does that make any sense? Like we didn't want to even contemplate that one of us could have done it.

SARAH. Well, of course, we still don't know who did do it.

GREG. I know, but really, it's probably somebody in his dorm. Don't you think?

SARAH. We really don't know yet.

GREG. Anyway, though, last night when Dean Strauss got up and said to, you know, look inside ourselves and see were we culpable at all, well, that's what really hit me, I guess. Because we still were acting like something outside was responsible. Instead of something inside. Which is what hit me. You know? It's in here. Inside.

SARAH. Well, I'm glad it started you thinking. That's what the meeting was for, I guess.

GREG. I think everyone came out of it really energized. I mean, just on my hall, we sat up until like three or four in the morning talking about it. About racism and how it had affected us, or not affected us as the case may be. I mean, where I'm from, I don't think people are racist. But then I didn't think anyone at Belmont was racist either.

SARAH. Where are you from?

GREG. Greenwich, Connecticut.

SARAH. Right.

GREG. But really, my point is that we were all geared up to talk last night, but today is another day and if we're not careful, we'll just drop it. So the thing is this: I want to start an organization. I want to call it Students for Tolerance. I want us to get together so we can keep talking like we were last night.

SARAH. I think that sounds like a fine idea.

GREG. Excellent! *(Small beat.)*

SARAH. So what would you like me to do for you, Greg?

GREG. Well, I thought I might go ahead and call a meeting for next week.

SARAH. Do you need a space?

GREG. That would be good.

SARAH *(opens a three-ring binder on her desk)*. You can have Scott Auditorium, Monday at seven.

GREG. Terrific. And I'd like to put up posters, announcing it.

SARAH. Go right ahead.

GREG. Well, this is what I was wondering. Is there any money the college could give us, to defray expenses?

SARAH. Of course. You'll need to go to the Student Activities Committee.

GREG. And they'll just give it to me?

SARAH. Well, you'll need to fill out some forms. You need to be approved as an official organization. And you'll need a sponsor. But I bet, if you asked Dean Strauss he'd be glad to sponsor you.

GREG. I don't know. This all seems so complicated all of a sudden.

SARAH. It's a little bit of work up front, but I think it's worth it.

GREG. You're right, of course. It's just...well, how long would it take to get funding?

SARAH. Probably six weeks.

GREG. Man.

SARAH. I know it seems like a long time, but if you wanted to go ahead and meet in the meantime, you can get the posters yourself and the committee will reimburse you. *(Beat.)* So if I were you, Greg, I'd go see Dean Strauss first. *(Beat.)*

GREG. This wouldn't...I mean, well, would it look bad if I said I was president of Students for Tolerance before the committee actually approved it?

SARAH. Bad to whom?

GREG. Well, I mean, to be perfectly honest, I'm applying to law school and the résumé is a little thin, if you know what I mean. I mean, something like this would definitely add a line.

SARAH. I see. *(Beat.)*

GREG. So do you think it would look bad?

SARAH. I really couldn't say. Would anyone question it?

GREG. I don't know. If they did, though, if they called the college ...

SARAH. I can't advise you on this, Greg. I think this is up to you to decide.

GREG. Oh. *(Beat.)* I mean, of course.

SARAH. I hope this doesn't dampen your enthusiasm for the idea.

GREG. Absolutely not. I'm committed to this. I am. Now if I can just figure out how to dig up some cash for these posters.

SARAH. Are you in a fraternity?

GREG. Yeah.

SARAH. Well, each fraternity's charter calls for a certain percentage of dues to be spent on service-oriented activities.

GREG. They do?

SARAH. Yes, they do. They could pay for your posters. *(Beat.)*

GREG. I don't know. It just doesn't seem like the kind of thing they'd go in for. I mean, would they even know what I was talking about? That's the question. Not to doubt you, of course, but I never heard of this fund or whatever before, and I actually manage to stay awake during those informational meetings. *(He laughs. SARAH doesn't.)*

SARAH. Greg, I'm intimately familiar with each fraternity's charter.

GREG. I'm sure you are. *(Beat.)* I mean, somebody around here is, obviously. Right? I mean, that's why we're going co-ed, isn't it?

SARAH. Yes. It is.

GREG *(laughs uncomfortably).* That was kind of a shock, when I first heard that. Co-ed fraternities. *(Beat.)* But really, the point was well taken. There are no sororities on campus. The women have no options. *(He laughs again, then studies SARAH.)* That was you, wasn't it, that started all the stir.

SARAH. Yes.

GREG. Dean Daniels. I'm sure I'd heard your name but I'd forgotten. Well. Congratulations on a job well done.

SARAH. Thank you.

GREG *(standing).* But rather than appeal to Tau Omega, I think I'll take your first piece of advice and go to the Student Activities Committee. I can wait. And I can shell out a few bucks for posters, too, if it's something I believe in.

SARAH. And you do.

GREG. And I do. *(Beat.)* Excellent, then. *(Offering his hand.)* You've been a great help. *(SARAH shakes his hand.)*

SARAH. That's why they pay me.

BLACKOUT

SCENE FOUR

Sarah's office, later that day. SARAH and ROSS are talking.

ROSS. Things just aren't the same. We're not communicating. At first I thought she just needed time, to readjust to being home, but it's been two weeks now and we've hardly had a conversation. Whenever I start talking to her, she just looks away and when I ask her what she's thinking about, she says, "Nothing."

SARAH. Did she meet somebody over in Europe?

ROSS. That's not what I'm saying.

SARAH. I was just thinking that maybe she had sex with somebody over in Europe and maybe she's thinking about that person she had sex with over in Europe.

ROSS. I thought you were willing to talk to me about this.

SARAH. I am. I'm talking to you.

ROSS. You're punishing me. This isn't how a friend would respond to my problems.

SARAH. Sorry. *(Beat.)* Maybe she's just pissed off that you had sex with somebody. Maybe you hurt her feelings.

ROSS. We had an agreement.

SARAH. Maybe she didn't actually expect you to take her up on it.

ROSS. You think she's jealous?

SARAH. I bet no matter what Petra says about the bourgeois restraints of traditional notions of commitment, or the bourgeois restraints of shoes, that she's pissed off and she's punishing you.

ROSS *(realizing it)*. She would never tell me if she was. She's really passive-aggressive.

SARAH. I can see why you like her.

ROSS *(changing the subject)*. All right then. Now, I'm supposed to reserve Ingersoll Chapel for our next forum.

SARAH. You are? *(She reaches for a binder.)*

ROSS. Tuesday night. I hope it's free because we've already posted it.

SARAH. I didn't realize you were having another one.

ROSS. Is it free?

SARAH. Yes. *(She makes a note.)* There. Tuesday night. Race forum.

ROSS. What's wrong?

SARAH. Nothing.

ROSS. You don't think we should have another one?

SARAH. I didn't say that.

ROSS. What then?

SARAH. I just think that if you're going to have another one, you should come up with a recommendation, or something, so that something tangible comes out of it instead of everybody standing around talking about how bad racism is. Because we already know that racism is bad.

ROSS. A recommendation?

SARAH. Yeah.

ROSS. Like what?

SARAH. I don't know. Stop being stupid.

ROSS. Stop being stupid?

SARAH. Yeah. Stop being stupid. Stop acting like you know the first thing about black people. Stop thinking you have black friends just because you got along really well with your nanny.

ROSS. That's what the forums are for, though. To help these kids understand a different range of experience.

SARAH. I'm sure that's your intent.

ROSS. But?

SARAH. But, in my humble opinion, all you do is talk about racism and then you heave this collective sigh of white guilt and then everybody feels better and then they drive downtown in their Saabs and buy sweaters.

ROSS. So you think the forums provide a sort of cheap penance?

SARAH. Yes.

ROSS. Well, I don't agree. I think they're very productive.

SARAH. Fine. I don't.

ROSS (*considers her*). You know, I like the way we're talking to each other. I think, maybe, when we were dating, you were holding back a little, avoiding conflict.

SARAH. Just out of some insane desire to get along.

ROSS. That's terrible.

SARAH. If it'll make you feel any better I'll drop all tact in the future.

ROSS. Excellent. Well, I'm off. (*He opens the door to leave. From off, we hear STRAUSS's voice.*)

STRAUSS (*off*). Ross!

ROSS. God. (*Muttering to SARAH.*) Ever since he had that thought piece published in the *Times*, he's just insufferable. (*To STRAUSS, off.*) Burton, hello!

(*STRAUSS appears at the door.*)

STRAUSS. Hello there. How are you?

ROSS. Fine.

STRAUSS. Did you see the latest *Harper's*?

ROSS. No, why?

STRAUSS. There was an article in there by David Foster. Wasn't he a classmate of yours?

ROSS. Yes. *(Beat.)* Was it any good?

STRAUSS. Quite good, really.

ROSS. Is he still harping on that authenticity thing?

STRAUSS. It was a piece on outsider art. Yes.

ROSS. Please.

STRAUSS. How are you, Sarah?

SARAH. Fine. Can I do something for you?

ROSS. I wonder if David's still fat.

STRAUSS. I need to talk to you both about something. *(He comes in and closes the door.)* This young man Greg Sullivan has approached me about sponsoring a Students for Tolerance group.

ROSS. What's this?

SARAH. A student group. For tolerance.

STRAUSS. It's an excellent idea, I think. A direct result of our forum. And I'm happy to do it, though really, Sarah, I was surprised that you recommended me.

SARAH. You seemed like an obvious choice to me.

STRAUSS. Well thank you. We're having our first meeting on Monday night, and the thing is this: we would like Simon Brick to attend.

SARAH. I don't think he can come.

STRAUSS. I understand that he's shy.

SARAH. He's quiet.

STRAUSS. But we're a small group and we would be honored to include him as a member.

SARAH. He didn't want to come to the forum, Burton. I doubt he'd want to come to this.

ROSS. I wish he had come.

SARAH. I supported his decision not to come.

STRAUSS. To whom?

SARAH. To him.

ROSS. I guess I can see how it might be intimidating, facing such a large crowd.

SARAH. I don't think it has anything to do with crowds.

ROSS. He's an only child, though, isn't he?

SARAH. I don't know.

STRAUSS. Maybe it's the cultural mix.

SARAH. What?

STRAUSS. He attended a predominantly African American school, didn't he? In Philadelphia?

ROSS. I thought he was from Bucks County.

SARAH. Pittsburgh. And I don't know what the racial mix was.

ROSS. But it was a public school.

SARAH. It was a Catholic school.

STRAUSS. Oh. I didn't realize he was Catholic.

SARAH. I don't know if he is or not. Is it important?

STRAUSS. No, no. Still, I'd like him to come.

ROSS. If Sarah's going to ask him to do something, she should ask him to come to the second forum.

STRAUSS. Ask him to do both. You could persuade him. You're very good with the students.

SARAH. Because I'm a social worker?

STRAUSS. What?

SARAH. Ayn Rand knew what to do with my sort. ...

STRAUSS (*laughs*). Oh. That. You didn't take me seriously did you?

SARAH. Yes.

STRAUSS. You don't really think that I subscribe to Ayn Rand? (*He laughs some more.*) Goodness. (*Beat.*)

SARAH. I'm not going to ask him to do anything, Burton. If it's so important to you, call him and ask him yourself.

STRAUSS. I suppose I could. I wonder, do they have their own phones now or would it ring in the hallway?

SARAH. They have their own phones. And electricity too.

STRAUSS. What?

ROSS. She's making a joke.

STRAUSS. Oh. You say he's very shy?

SARAH. No. He's quiet but I don't think he's shy.

STRAUSS. Maybe we could write him a note.

SARAH. You should do that, then. *(A knock on the door.)* Yes?

(MR. MEYERS enters.)

MEYERS. I'm sorry. I didn't realize you had company.

SARAH. It's all right. We're finished.

STRAUSS *(to ROSS)*. Do you want to help me write a note?

ROSS. I'd be glad to. Thanks, Sarah.

SARAH. Sure.

(They leave. MEYERS closes the door behind them).

MEYERS. Simon got another one. *(He pulls a note from his pocket and hands it to SARAH.)*

SARAH *(looking at the note, reading)*. "Little Black Sambo..." *(Beat.)* God. Is he in his room now? *(MEYERS nods.)* Let's take this to Dean Kenney and then I'll go talk to him.

MEYERS. Okay.

(They turn to leave when PATRICK enters the open door.)

MEYERS. Hi, Patrick.

PATRICK. Could I talk to you?

SARAH. This is kind of a bad time. Can we make it tomorrow?

PATRICK. My dad said I should insist on talking to you. Now.

SARAH. Okay. *(SARAH looks at MEYERS.)*

MEYERS. I'll wait outside.

SARAH. Thank you.

(MEYERS exits, closing the door behind him.)

PATRICK. We got this letter from the financial aid office. *(He holds out a letter to SARAH. Before she can take it:)* When I got the scholarship they took away my financial aid. It's costing more now.

SARAH. That's not right. Let me see.

PATRICK. My dad is furious. He was already mad about the whole Hispanic thing.

SARAH. He was?

PATRICK. Yeah, but I told him that you were just...you know, trying to help us out. That it wasn't you, it was these other people who didn't get it, but he said I shouldn't have to make compromises to get something.

SARAH. Would you like me to talk to him? Maybe I could explain it to him.

PATRICK. I don't know. He was totally pissed and then I told him about the thing with Simon Brick and he completely freaked.

SARAH. Oh.

PATRICK. Yeah. He said that's exactly why he didn't want me to come here.

SARAH. Your father didn't want you to come here?

PATRICK. No. It was my decision, but he didn't want me to. So now I gotta fix this thing with my financial aid because my dad was already complaining about how much this place costs, and now he can't believe it.

SARAH. Stop worrying. I'll take care of it. You deserve that scholarship and I'm going to straighten this out. Okay?

PATRICK. Okay. *(Beat. He doesn't leave.)*

SARAH. What is it?

PATRICK. Well, some of my friends asked me to talk to you about something else.

SARAH. Yeah?

PATRICK. We felt like that meeting thing we had to go to was really insulting.

SARAH. The forum?

PATRICK. Yeah. We felt like it was really patronizing. You know?

SARAH. You mean the minority students?

PATRICK. No. I mean ... what? Do you think all my friends are minority students?

SARAH. Of course not. I just thought that's what you meant.

PATRICK. Why? Because "Hispanic" people stick together?

SARAH. No, I just ... I didn't ... I wasn't thinking, like, you and your "amigos" or anything. *(She laughs.)* That was a joke. I was making a joke.

PATRICK. It wasn't funny.

SARAH. God, Patrick, I'm sorry. Let's start over. You said the forum was patronizing and I thought, "To whom would it be most patronizing?" and then I thought, "To the minority students," and so I said that. Because it was patronizing. To the minority students.

PATRICK. You know, I didn't correct you before, when I was in here before, but it's "students of color," not "minority students."

SARAH. Students of color. God. Sorry. Of course. That's what I meant to say. The "minority" thing, it's just a technical thing.

PATRICK. What does that mean?

SARAH. Just, you know, paperwork... everything has to fit into a box. It's an administrative thing.

PATRICK. So is that why you made me say I was Puerto Rican?

SARAH *(beat)*. You know, Patrick, I wasn't trying to make you say anything, really. I thought I explained. How it would make it easier to get the scholarship. That's all it was. I just wanted to make sure you got the scholarship.

PATRICK. So it was a compromise.

SARAH. Yes. *(Quickly.)* And no. No, not a compromise like your dad meant, in a bad way, but a good compromise between the two of us. That you agreed to.

PATRICK. Right.

SARAH *(beat)*. So why did you find the forum patronizing?

PATRICK. Well, because. The students of color were being talked about like we weren't even there, like we couldn't even talk for ourselves. And the white kids were being talked about like they were all criminals. I mean, I think Dean Strauss managed to offend everybody in the audience. *(SARAH laughs.)* You were up there too, on stage.

SARAH. But I didn't say anything.

PATRICK. But you were up there.

SARAH. Right. *(Beat.)* So essentially, you felt you were being robbed of your agency.

PATRICK. I probably wouldn't use that particular expression, like that. But I'd say yeah. Basically it felt like I didn't exist.

SARAH. So, would you feel comfortable saying that? At the next forum?

PATRICK. They're gonna have another one?

SARAH. Tuesday night. Why don't you go?

PATRICK. I don't know.

SARAH. Look, the faculty have definitely had their say. I think it's time for them to listen to the students, don't you? *(PATRICK doesn't answer.)* You should tell Dean Strauss how he made you feel. Otherwise he'll never know that it's wrong. *(Beat.)*

PATRICK. Maybe I will go.

SARAH. Good. *(Beat.)* Now about the scholarship, just tell your father that he doesn't have to worry. I'll take care of it. Tell him you'll be paying less than you would at a state school.

PATRICK. I'll tell him that.

SARAH. He should be very proud of you. There aren't many scholarships this size. It's really an honor. *(PATRICK nods, unimpressed.)* Look, Patrick, I really am on your side. You're an exceptional student and you're obviously very smart and very talented. I'm sorry if I've offended you.

PATRICK. You've apologized already.

SARAH. And as my dad used to say, "You can't put that in the bank."

PATRICK. That's not what I meant.

SARAH *(quickly)*. No, it's okay if you did. It's okay. So let me give you twelve thousand dollars. Because that's something you can put in the bank. Okay?

PATRICK *(beat. Accepting it)*. Okay.

BLACKOUT

SCENE FIVE

Sarah's office, the next week. She is on the phone.

SARAH *(on phone).* I guess, I mean, if you wanted to eat waffles in the middle of the day, I don't see anything wrong with that. *(Beat.)* Well yeah, I would say heat them up at least. *(Beat.)* I'm fine...*(Beat. Different tone.)* I am. It's just...it seems like, you know, I keep calling you earlier in the day, and you're drinking earlier in the day. *(Beat.)* Well we had a deal, you know, that we wouldn't talk when you were drunk and now I'm wondering, you know, when is that?...What's that beeping?...Well don't answer it....I don't care, let them call back—Mom!—

(She puts the phone back to her ear, resigned to waiting. STRAUSS knocks on the door and sticks his head in.)

I'm on the phone.

STRAUSS. It's really urgent.

SARAH. I'm on the phone.

STRAUSS. Simon Brick must come to the next forum.

SARAH. So you can yell at him?

STRAUSS. None of that would have happened last night if Simon had been there.

SARAH. I don't follow. *(Back in phone, quickly, she holds up her hand to STRAUSS to get him to shut up. Trying to keep her voice low:)* Are you there? *(Beat. In phone.)* Well why did you tell her. Don't tell her what I said. *(Beat. In phone.)* Can I call you later? *(Beat.)* Okay. I—

(Beat.) No, I'm sorry. *(Beat. In phone.)* I love you too. *(She hangs up.)*

STRAUSS. Family?

SARAH. My mother.

STRAUSS. I could tell. I'm the same way with my mother. It's like I'm twelve again. *(Beat. They study each other.)*

SARAH. I'm sorry, Burton, what did you want?

STRAUSS. I just feel that the students wouldn't have attacked me if Simon had been there.

SARAH. How could Simon have prevented it?

STRAUSS. If he were there and they could see that I support him and they could see ...

SARAH. A black person on stage with you?

STRAUSS. A united front.

SARAH. Well, that might be part of the problem, but I think an even larger part is that you yelled at them. They were just trying to explain their feelings and you lit into them.

STRAUSS. They were questioning my motivations! My intentions!

SARAH. All they said was that your manner was patronizing.

STRAUSS. Which implies that I'm racist! *(Beat.)* This is very upsetting to me.

SARAH. I can see that.

STRAUSS. I've never been criticized like this before.

SARAH. Well, I don't think that it was completely outrageous.

STRAUSS. Oh?

SARAH. Well, you do have a kind of "Old World" manner about you. You know?

STRAUSS. Oh, this is precious.

SARAH. Not to hurt your feelings, but...

STRAUSS. Coming from you!

SARAH. What's that supposed to mean?

STRAUSS. You're a goddamned bureaucrat! A clerk!

SARAH. I'm sorry?

STRAUSS. "Have a nice day." "Come back and see us."
  You may as well be working at a bank!

SARAH (*stares, befuddled*). I just... how did we get here?

STRAUSS. I want Simon Brick!

SARAH. Then ask him!

STRAUSS. He wouldn't answer our note!

SARAH. Then leave him alone!

(DEAN KENNEY comes in.)

KENNEY. What is all the yelling?

STRAUSS. I need her help, she won't give it to me.

KENNEY. What do you need, Burton?

STRAUSS. I need Simon Brick to come to the forum, to
  tell them I'm not a racist.

KENNEY. I don't think that's a good idea.

STRAUSS. But I—

KENNEY. I know you're upset but it's never a good idea
  to let someone else speak for you. You have to explain
  to them who you are. They don't know your history or
  your record. How hard you've fought for them over the
  years. (*Small beat.*)

STRAUSS. They don't know that I'm the sponsor of Students for Tolerance.

KENNEY. Exactly. You know what you should do? You
  should go back to your office and clear your head, and
  write down what you want to say to them. (*He consid-*

ers.) You don't need anybody to defend you, Burton. It's ridiculous to think that you do.

STRAUSS. You're right. I don't know what got into me. I don't know what I thought Sarah could do.

KENNEY. Well, she's our liaison to the minority students. You thought she could help. But you don't need anyone's help. That's my point.

STRAUSS *(gives a little giggle).* I get so worked up.

KENNEY. I know you do.

STRAUSS. All right, Catherine. Thank you. *(He gives her a peck on the cheek and hurries off.)*

SARAH. What was that about?

KENNEY. Burton and I, you know, have had something of a tortured relationship for a long while. It ceased to be sexual some time ago, but we still have deep feelings for one another. I think I may be the only person in the world who fully understands him. He's very vulnerable. *(Pause. SARAH stares.)*

SARAH. I just meant, what was that about my being a liaison to the minority students.

KENNEY. Oh. Well, because of the Lancaster thing.

SARAH. Pardon?

KENNEY. Well, you know we consciously set out to diversify and we really wanted your experience, coming from Lancaster. Serving a more ... diverse student population.

SARAH. It wasn't really diverse.

KENNEY. Then a minority population.

SARAH. *I* was in the minority.

KENNEY. Then an African American population. Is that what you want me to say?

SARAH. I don't want you to say anything. It's just that, it was a fluke that I was there in the first place. They needed a last-minute replacement. My dissertation advisor recommended me.

KENNEY. But you must have specialized, or expressed an interest ...

SARAH. So you wanted someone who had worked with students of color.

KENNEY. Yes.

SARAH. That was never made clear to me. *(Beat.)* Why didn't you hire a black person then?

KENNEY. Well ... I'll be honest, we did try.

SARAH. You couldn't get anybody.

KENNEY. We had someone in mind but he took another offer. I think he wanted more money. And I don't think he really wanted to live in Vermont.

SARAH. I did want to live in Vermont.

KENNEY. We're a good match then. *(Starts to leave.)*

SARAH. So when I came here for my interview, were you surprised?

KENNEY. Surprised?

SARAH. Because I was white?

KENNEY. Oh. No.

SARAH. So you didn't think, that because I'd been at Lancaster, that I was black?

KENNEY. No.

SARAH. Really?

KENNEY *(beat)*. Well, we did. But of course, you weren't, and of course, we knew you weren't when we hired you. So don't let it bother you. *(SARAH laughs.)* What?

SARAH. Nothing. So how many people did you fly in for interviews?

KENNEY. Three, including you.

SARAH. What was wrong with the other person?

KENNEY. Nothing. We really shouldn't be talking about this.

SARAH. Did I ask for less?

KENNEY. Sarah! This isn't really appropriate. You know? I never should have brought it up.

SARAH. I brought it up.

KENNEY. That's right. You never should have brought it up. *(Beat.)* So have you gotten those handwriting samples to the FBI?

SARAH. I'm working on it.

KENNEY. Good, I want to get this over with. *(She gives an awkward laugh.)* I mean the whole thing is giving me a headache.

BLACKOUT

SCENE SIX

Sarah's office, the next day. PATRICK CHIBAS stands before Sarah's desk. He holds a copy of the student newspaper. He is waiting impatiently. SARAH enters with MR. MEYERS.

SARAH *(seeing PATRICK)*. Hi, Patrick, hang on a minute. *(She crosses to her desk and pulls out a manila envelope.)* I did what they said and made a key, so the samples are just numbered and the key shows whose handwriting it is.

MEYERS. Okay.

SARAH. And do you know when ... ?

MEYERS. Couple of weeks? I don't know.

SARAH. Okay, thanks. *(MEYERS leaves, closing the door behind him. To PATRICK.)* Sorry about the wait. Did you get a letter from financial aid? I cleared up your scholarship. *(Pause. PATRICK studies her.)* Your father should be happy.

PATRICK. You wanted to talk to me about my editorial, didn't you?

SARAH. That was ... yes.

PATRICK. Am I not allowed to express my opinions now? Is that it?

SARAH. No. That's not it. You just raised some serious allegations and I thought we should discuss them. *(Small beat.)* Because part of this is about me. Right?

PATRICK. Part of it. I guess. I mean, obviously, most of it is about Dean Strauss.

SARAH. But this part ... *(She picks up her own copy of the paper and reads.)* "The racist attitude of the administration goes beyond Dean Strauss, however. Many students have experienced discrimination by the college. One student says she was asked in her sociology class to give the 'African American point of view.' Another says he was offered a minority scholarship, then—when his own ethnicity was found to be unacceptable—he was given a list of 'official' minorities to pick from, as if any one would do. This treatment reeks of tokenism and is an insult to the achievements of all students of color at Belmont."

PATRICK *(beat)*. I didn't mention you by name.

SARAH. I appreciate that, I guess.

PATRICK. Do you want to know why?

SARAH. Why?

PATRICK. It's because I sat here and took it from you. Twice. For twelve thousand dollars.

SARAH. No you didn't.

PATRICK. Yes I did.

SARAH. Patrick, I wasn't saying to you that Nuyorican was somehow an "unacceptable" thing to be. Did you really think I was saying that?

PATRICK. Yes. And I tried to tell you and you didn't listen. And then I gave up. And I let you put down Puerto Rican, but I've never even been to Puerto Rico.

SARAH. I never would have put that down if I didn't think it was all right with you. Do you understand that?

PATRICK. All I know is that you're the dean. And if I want something, I have to do what you say. (Pause.)

SARAH. I didn't know you felt that way. I'm sorry I didn't make myself clearer. But I really just wanted to do right by you. It was important to me to see that you got that scholarship. Which you did.

PATRICK. But why does it have to come at a price? Why is there always some fucking price?

SARAH. I thought...I was working hard to make the college pay you something. I wanted the price to be in their debit column. Do you see?

PATRICK. No.

SARAH. See, I used to work for this very poor, inner-city college with no money for anybody and I couldn't give anybody scholarships, and when I got here and saw what I could do, you know, how much money there was and how I could just fix some things, like the fraternities, you know...how I made them co-ed?

PATRICK. I'm not in a fraternity.

SARAH. I know you're not. I just thought I could make amends somehow, in a tangible way. Do you know what I mean?

PATRICK. No.

SARAH. I just wanted you to get that scholarship. I thought you'd, you know, take it and go on to solve the red tide or save the rain forest or something.

PATRICK. What?

SARAH. That you'd take it and solve the red tide. *(Beat.)*

PATRICK. You don't know what I want to do. Do you? *(Beat.)*

SARAH. I don't know, I guess I...I guess I don't. I guess I wasn't paying attention to the details of your composition.

PATRICK. What does that mean? "The details of my composition."

SARAH. I wasn't paying attention to who you are.

PATRICK. No shit. *(Pause. SARAH looks a little sickened.)*

SARAH. You know, Patrick, I'm afraid it's a hazard of the job...sometimes I slip into a certain way of speaking, or relating to people—*(Laughs.)* Like that. "Relating to people." You know? I don't normally talk like that, but so many people come in and you talk to so many students—so I guess I'm saying, that without realizing it, even in spite of your best intentions, sometimes you start to talk to people like you're a bank clerk.

PATRICK. I don't think this is my problem. Whatever it is you're talking about.

SARAH. I'm just trying to explain.

PATRICK. But it's not my problem. And the thing is you haven't once listened to what my problem is.

SARAH. I have.

PATRICK. No you haven't. Nobody's listened to me. You told me I should go to that forum and Dean Strauss would listen to me but I barely got two words out before he started yelling at me. In front of the entire school he stood up there and yelled at me like I was some sort of idiot.

SARAH. That was a knee-jerk reaction on his part. He wasn't yelling at you. He doesn't even know you.

PATRICK. Then who was he yelling at? I mean, I was the one standing there. I was the one standing there for ten minutes while he went off. I was the one who felt like an idiot.

SARAH. But you know you're not an idiot. You shouldn't let his—

PATRICK. It doesn't matter now because I'm applying to NYU for the spring. Okay? I'm not staying here.

SARAH. Patrick!

PATRICK. I hate this place. You know? You can give me twelve thousand dollars and I don't care. It's not worth it. My father says if I stay here, all I'll learn is shame.

SARAH. That's not all you'll learn.

PATRICK (*overriding her*). Also, I should tell you that I sent a letter to President Garvey telling him I'm transferring and saying that this is pretty much why.

SARAH. I wish you would take some time. I know you're angry, but I wish you'd take some time and reconsider.

PATRICK. I hate Vermont. (*He starts to leave.*)

SARAH. Patrick...!

PATRICK (*stops*). What.

SARAH. I feel like I've failed you. I'm sorry.

PATRICK. I don't know, Dean Daniels. You just keep apologizing all the time, like you want me to pass my

hand over your head and make it all better. You know?
Like I'm a saint, or something.

SARAH. I don't, really.

PATRICK. I'm not a saint.

SARAH. No. You're just a kid.

PATRICK. I'm not a kid, either. I mean, I'm right here in
front of you. Are you even looking at me?

SARAH. I am. And I see a very smart young man who—

PATRICK *(overlapping, starting to leave)*. Forget it.

SARAH. Who should reconsider because it's ridiculous to
let your talent go to waste—

PATRICK *(interrupting)*. I don't want to reconsider and I
don't want any more compliments! I'm not some genius
or something. I'm just whatever I am and I just want to
go someplace where I won't stand out! *(Opening the
door.)*

SARAH. Patrick—!

PATRICK. I don't want to discuss it, I just want to go! *(He
leaves, slamming the door behind him.)*

SARAH *(almost to herself)*. Patrick. *(Beat.)* I'm sorry.

END OF ACT ONE

ACT TWO

SCENE ONE

AT RISE: *Sarah's office, a few hours later. It is nighttime.*

ROSS. You know, I grew up on a farm. I had a rural experience. But now I'm very much a part of the institution, so how could I call myself an outsider?

SARAH. I don't know.

ROSS. Me neither. But Foster's argument is that any expression that challenges the "establishment"—and that's actually the word he used, the "establishment"—whether it originates from a formally trained artist or not, constitutes "outsider" art. So by his definition, I could make outsider art.

SARAH. I don't even know what outsider art is.

ROSS. Well, it's just a fancy term for folk art.

SARAH. So what's wrong with saying folk art.

ROSS. I guess people thought it was diminutive.

SARAH. How?

ROSS. Well, to be a folk artist is to be untrained, which usually entails being disadvantaged. Economically, I mean. And undereducated.

SARAH. Or uneducated.

ROSS. Undereducated, I guess, is the preferred term.

SARAH. So, it's just art made by poor stupid people.

ROSS. Well, if you want to be rude about it.

SARAH. So my family could make outsider art. If any of them wanted to change hobbies and give up drinking. *(Beat.)*

ROSS. Are you okay?

SARAH. I don't know. Lately, I look around here, and I feel like I don't live up to the architecture. All the granite. The white columns. The blue shutters and slate roofs. It's all so ... college-y.

ROSS. I like Belmont. I've always thought it was very pleasing to the eye.

SARAH. But doesn't it ever make you feel ugly?

ROSS. Ugly how?

SARAH. Like being ugly, like saying ugly things? Sometimes I want to run out onto the quad and hike up my skirt and pee all over everything.

ROSS. See, I think that you're so conditioned to repressing your feelings that natural anger or frustration gets channeled until you can't help but express it in some inappropriate way. If you were a painter you could be a Jackson Pollock and let your rage fly out onto the canvas but you're not, you're a ...

SARAH. Administrator.

ROSS. Administrator and so you ...

SARAH. Pee all over the grass.

ROSS. Right.

SARAH. But I'm a person, too. You know? I'm not an object. To be studied. I'm not the subject of a painting. I'm not here to be aestheticized.

ROSS. Why do you say that?

SARAH. I think that's what you do. You make everyone the subject of a lecture.

ROSS. I do not.

SARAH. Yes you do.

ROSS. No I don't.

SARAH *(quoting)*. "There was this man on the train and his shirt cuffs were frayed and his shoe leather was cracked and he held this card before him like a beacon..." *(Beat.)*

ROSS. What is your point?

SARAH. I don't think poverty is romantic.

ROSS. I wasn't romanticizing him. I was trying to understand him.

SARAH. You were idealizing him.

ROSS. Because I thought he seemed strong?

SARAH. Yes.

ROSS. But he was so neatly dressed, and so focused. He seemed strong. What's wrong with that?

SARAH. You idealized him and that means that you didn't respect him.

ROSS. What?

SARAH. To idealize is to fundamentally mark as different; it is not to respect. It is to fundamentally mark as different and therefore, not equal. So that man on the train could never be your equal.

ROSS. Sure he could.

SARAH. No he couldn't.

ROSS. You can't assume that. He may be my equal. I don't know. I don't know him. If I got to know him then maybe we could find that out.

SARAH. No, there's no objective measurement of whether or not he's your equal. That's not my point. I'm saying that you're not *allowing* him to be your equal.

ROSS. I might if I knew him.

SARAH. But you'll never get to know him. He's a poor
crazy man. You'll always just stare at him on the train.
You idealize him or you denigrate him, but either way
you see him as fundamentally different. He is not your
equal, you cannot respect him.

ROSS. I can.

SARAH. No you can't.

ROSS. I can.

SARAH. No you can't.

ROSS. Why are you insisting on this?

SARAH. It's important.

ROSS. To you?

SARAH. Yes. *(Beat.)* I screwed up this kid's scholarship.

ROSS. What?

SARAH. I screwed up this kid's scholarship. I thought, if I
was up-front about it, then it wouldn't be wrong because
I thought, maybe we were in on it together but of course
the balance of power was off and so he wasn't "in" on
anything. You know? But I thought that he was a genius,
and that he would solve the red tide and save the mana-
tees. But I didn't know the first thing about him, and I
screwed it up.

ROSS. I didn't understand anything you just said.

SARAH. I...nothing. *(Beat.)* To idealize is not to respect.
(Beat.) Why aren't you home with Petra?

ROSS. She has a rehearsal tonight.

SARAH. For the fall dance recital.

ROSS. Right. Are you going?

SARAH. No. I just approved the funds for the posters. I
don't really like dance. Everybody all "in tune" with
their bodies. I think the whole mind/body dichotomy
should be given another chance.

ROSS *(beat)*. I don't know, Sarah. Sometimes, I think you focus on the negative aspects of every situation. You're very cynical.

SARAH. Great.

ROSS. What?

SARAH. It's just a constant refrain. Sooner or later everybody tells me I'm cynical.

ROSS. How do you respond?

SARAH. I don't think I'm cynical. I think I'm honest.

ROSS. But you're not. You're withholding something.

SARAH. Why do you say that?

ROSS. I don't know. I just feel it. *(Beat.)* You're equivocating.

BLACKOUT

SCENE TWO

Sarah's office, a few days later. SARAH isn't there but STRAUSS is sitting in the office, anyway, reading a typewritten manuscript. KENNEY walks in briskly.

KENNEY. Where is she?

STRAUSS. I don't know.

KENNEY. What are you doing here?

STRAUSS. You were right, Catherine. I cleared my head and wrote down what I wanted to say. *(He hands her the manuscript.)* My mea culpa.

KENNEY. What?

STRAUSS. I want to tell the students I'm sorry. They were right. Over the years, without realizing it, I assimilated. I adopted the attributes of the dominant class in order to succeed in a world that was not my own. It was Sarah who made me realize it. She said I had an "Old World" manner.

KENNEY. Oh for God's sake. You went to Groton.

STRAUSS. Precisely.

(SARAH enters, carrying a take-out bag.)

Sarah, I've come to thank you. You made me realize why the students misread me.

SARAH. I did?

STRAUSS. Here's an advance copy of the talk I've prepared for tonight's forum. Feel free to jot notes in the margins.

SARAH. I might not have time to read it.

STRAUSS. Then keep it for your records. *(She takes it.)* What is that in the bag?

SARAH. My lunch.

STRAUSS. What is it?

SARAH. A tuna salad sandwich. *(Beat.)* And chips.

STRAUSS. On rye?

SARAH. On raisin bread, actually.

STRAUSS. Really? I've never tried it. Is it good?

SARAH. Yeah. You can get one at the cafeteria.

STRAUSS. Excellent, I'll try it. Catherine, good day. *(He exits. Beat.)*

SARAH. It's nice to see Burton getting down with the people.

KENNEY *(ignoring her)*. President Garvey called and he's gotten a letter from this Patrick Chibas student. Do you know about this?

SARAH. Yes.

KENNEY. President Garvey is very upset. He says all we're doing is sowing racial discord, not racial harmony, and what do we plan to do about it? *(Beat.)* So? What do we plan to do about it?

SARAH. I don't know.

KENNEY. Sarah.

SARAH. I don't. I'm sorry.

KENNEY. Well you better come up with something because that's why we hired you. So here's what I want. I want a ten-point plan with specific, concrete suggestions that don't involve a lot of funding but will have a great impact. And I want you to type it up so that any idiot can understand it. Type it up in a bulleted list.

SARAH. A bulleted list?

KENNEY. Yes. A list with bullets to the side.

SARAH *(overlapping)*. I know what a bulleted list is.

KENNEY. Then what?

SARAH. You want me to solve racism with a bulleted list?

KENNEY. Garvey is livid! The board is livid and I can't blame them. This Patrick Chibas could go to the press!

SARAH. He won't.

KENNEY. We're already in the Boston papers. Are you aware of that?

SARAH. No.

KENNEY. "Racial incident at Belmont." "Racists run Belmont ragged."

SARAH. It didn't really say that, did it?

KENNEY. It was the gist! The gist! We never should have started all this goddamn dialogue. This was an internal affair until you called the police.

SARAH *(beat)*. When do you want the list?

KENNEY. Tomorrow.

SARAH. Tomorrow? We've got a stupid forum tonight.

KENNEY. If you start whining, Sarah, I'll ask someone else to do it.

SARAH. I am not whining.

KENNEY. Fine.

SARAH. I—*(There's a knock at the door.)*

KENNEY. You what?

(MR. MEYERS pokes his head in.)

MEYERS. Sarah? *(Sees KENNEY.)* Oh, excuse me.

KENNEY. Come in, I have to go anyway. *(To SARAH.)* I'll come by in the morning.
(She exits. MEYERS closes the door behind her, then walks over to Sarah's desk with a rock.)

SARAH. What's this?

MEYERS. Somebody threw a rock through Simon's window.

SARAH. Oh my God. Is he all right?

MEYERS. He's fine. Holding up.

SARAH. Did he see anything?

MEYERS. Came home from classes, there it was.

SARAH. Who is doing this?

MEYERS. I wish I knew. Listen, Simon asked me to ask you not to tell his parents about this. He said they'd make him come home.

SARAH. They're very worried.

MEYERS. I bet.

SARAH. I can't really lie to them, though.

MEYERS. I'm not telling you what to do. I'm just passing that along.

SARAH. I'll go talk to him. *(Small beat.)* Or no, better yet, I'll call a campus-wide meeting and put it up for a vote. *(Beat. MEYERS stares at her.)* Nobody laughs at my jokes.

MEYERS. That was a joke?

SARAH. Yes!

MEYERS. Sorry. It's hard to tell these days.

BLACKOUT

SCENE THREE

Sarah's office, much later that night. She works by the light of a lamp. She is struggling with her bulleted list. There is a knock at the door which startles her. She yells.

SARAH. Who is it?

ROSS *(off)*. Ross.

SARAH. Come in.

(He enters.)

ROSS. What are you doing here so late?

SARAH. What are you doing here so late?

ROSS. I was taking a walk.

SARAH. What's wrong?

ROSS. Petra and I had a big fight.

SARAH. So was I right? Was she mad at you for sleeping around?

ROSS. I didn't sleep around. I slept with you.

SARAH. But was she mad?

ROSS. Yes.

SARAH. Ha. Radicals.

ROSS. Don't sneer.

SARAH. Did you apologize?

ROSS. Yes.

SARAH. Did you follow your apology with, "But we had an agreement."

ROSS *(reluctantly)*. Yes.

SARAH. Maybe you should leave that out, next time.

ROSS. It doesn't matter. We always fight.

SARAH. Because you're so passionate?

ROSS. No. I used to think we were passionate. Now I just think we're incompatible. *(Small beat.)* I'm tired.

SARAH. I'm sorry.

ROSS. It's okay. It's my own fault. *(Changing the subject.)* So what are you doing up here so late?

SARAH. Making a bulleted list.

ROSS. Of course. For what?

SARAH. Catherine wants a plan. She wants to know how we can fix the racial discord we've sown.

ROSS. *We've* sown? I love that. It's her complete lack of understanding. It's Burton's ridiculous posturing. That forum tonight was a laughing stock. That thing Burton read? Jesus. *(He laughs.)* Just because he didn't make the lacrosse team at Groton he had to "assimilate."

SARAH. At least nobody was there to hear it.

ROSS. It was rather sparsely attended, wasn't it.

SARAH. The Black Student Union was boycotting.

ROSS. They were?

SARAH. Didn't you notice that there were just a lot of white people there?

ROSS. Well, yes. But, I mean, even when everyone's there, there's still just a lot of white people. I didn't know we were being boycotted.

SARAH. Yes.

ROSS. I had no idea. *(Beat.)* Then maybe Catherine's right? We should make a list. A plan. That's what you suggested in the first place, wasn't it?

SARAH. Back when I thought I had a clue.

ROSS. So what have you got so far? *(SARAH hands him a notepad. He reads the first page.)* "One. Stop being stupid." Sarah. "Two. Move to Vermont." What does that mean?

SARAH. Just that, you know, if you don't like black people, moving to Vermont can take care of that. Because there aren't any black people here.

ROSS. "Three. Admit defeat." Sarah. You shouldn't do things like this.

SARAH. Why not?

ROSS. Because it sounds terrible.

SARAH. Well I'm just being honest.

ROSS *(pause).* You know, I really wonder about you sometimes.

SARAH. I have moments, is all.

ROSS. Moments of what?

SARAH. Moments of despair. *(Beat.)*

ROSS. That kid that you were telling me about, whose scholarship you screwed up, that was Patrick Chibas, wasn't it?

SARAH. Yes.

ROSS. He is one of my students. My survey class. That's why I didn't recognize him. He came by today and told me he's transferring.

SARAH. Yeah.

ROSS. I read his editorial, I...I just didn't put it together. So you thought he would do something with the red tide?

SARAH. I thought I would help him. The way I used to think I would help people. *(Beat.)* I don't know what I was thinking. I've really regressed.

ROSS. How's that?

SARAH. I...when I went to graduate school, I really wanted to go into administration because I had this misguided desire to help people.

ROSS. Misguided how?

SARAH. You know, like a missionary, or something.

ROSS. Is that what you were doing with Patrick?

SARAH. I don't know. I didn't think I was. I thought I was just being upfront. Pragmatic. You know? I thought pragmatism was a potential cure. Like, maybe I couldn't have the right attitude, but at least I could give twelve thousand dollars to somebody who needed it. But I couldn't even do that right.

ROSS. What do you mean, the right attitude?

SARAH. Well...you know.

ROSS. No I don't.

SARAH. Just the racial thing.

ROSS. What racial thing.

SARAH. That thing. You know. The thing. Where you do the whole thing and then you have the right attitude.

ROSS. What whole thing?

SARAH. The moment of realization. The guilt. The transformation. *(He looks to her for an explanation.)* The thing, where you think you're not racist and then you learn how you are racist. And then you stop being a racist. *(ROSS waits.)* Like, maybe you think you're really liberal so you decide to go into some field where you can help minority students. So you go to graduate school. But when you get there, you meet people who are a lot smarter than you, and also a lot more abrasive than you, and they point out that your desire to help minority students doesn't have anything to do with a sense of justice or fair play. Instead it stems from your "plantation mentality." Your paternalism. Your desire to help the noble savage.

ROSS. You actually thought about it in those terms?

SARAH. Not consciously, no. But that's what I learned. I learned that I was thinking in those terms. When I got to graduate school. From those people. Who were so much smarter than me.

ROSS. So you were enlightened?

SARAH. That's what I was aiming for. Enlightenment. Definitely. I went to seminars in the education department. I took every class on African American literature and theory I could find. I read all this stuff I'd never read before. The whole shebang from Frederick Douglass to Henry Louis Gates Jr. to bell hooks. I wanted to hear the African American voice and the African American viewpoint. And I listened and I absorbed because I was scared shitless to actually say anything. Because what I learned real fast was that I was the one. It was me. I was the one who had kept black people down. Or if not me, personally, then I was still responsible by proxy.

ROSS. Are you being sarcastic?

SARAH. No, I really, I felt...I felt terrible. Everything I read indicted me. I wanted to apologize to the entire race and empty my pockets and say, "Here! Take it! Take it! What's mine is yours! Take it! I'm sorry! I'm so so sorry!" Hell, by the time we read *Native Son* I was so worked up I was convinced somebody was going to kill me in my bed and chop me up and shove me in a furnace, but I didn't care, because I deserved it. I was Mary Dalton. I was the naive white girl. "Chop me up! Shove me in a furnace and when you sift through the ashes and find my bones wear them on a chain around your neck and dance the dance of the righteous for you are good and I am bad!"

ROSS. Maybe you were missing the point...

SARAH. No. I got the point. I just still thought it was all about me, you see. I cherished how badly I felt. I had been a racist. And I had repented.

ROSS. You shouldn't be so hard on yourself. Maybe some of your motivations were selfish, but you confronted the worst in yourself.

SARAH. No. It was a false conversion. *(Beat.)* You see, I'm afraid I'm going to start the whole thing over again.

ROSS. What thing?

SARAH. The thing that happened at Lancaster. What if it happens here, with Hispanics. Or Nuyoricans. Or whatever.

ROSS. What do you mean?

SARAH. I came here to get away from Lancaster. *(Beat.)* Because I hated Lancaster.

ROSS. What?

SARAH. It made me worse. *(Small beat. Calm.)* I mean, before I was just paternalistic. Now, I'm fully aware that black people have agency and are responsible and can help themselves, but I think they don't do it because they're lazy and stupid.

ROSS. Sarah!

SARAH. So back then, when I thought I had learned my lesson, I hadn't. I haven't. All I learned was how to appreciate black people. The way you might appreciate a painting or a good bottle of Bordeaux. I studied them to figure them out. Like Sanskrit. But that's no different from hating them.

ROSS. Oh, for God's sake.

SARAH. It's not.

ROSS. It is!

SARAH. It's called objectification, Ross. And it relies on keeping the object of your investigation at bay. It relies on knowing one or two really well-educated black people. Because when you come face to face with a lot of just regular black people, you can't aestheticize them anymore. They're too damn scary.

ROSS. Jesus, Sarah.

SARAH *(without apology. Very straightforward).* Look, this is... I've been struggling with this for a long, long time. I have. I thought I was fine, I thought I was making progress until I got that job at Lancaster. I thought I was fine. But then I had to move to Chicago and I don't know. Everything seemed different. All my newfound self-awareness and societal insight and... and all that crap, all that crap just flew out the window. So quickly. Because in the abstract, black people were fine. But in reality, they were so rude. And it wasn't my first expo-

sure, you know, to a black population. I'd lived in a big
city before. But my relationship with them was different
this time. They weren't serving me anymore. I was serving them.

ROSS. At Lancaster?

SARAH. Yes. I shouldn't have been there and I knew I
shouldn't have been there and I occasionally apologized
for being there. But I still thought I could do a good job.
And then I met the students. *(Beat.)* And they were all
black. Of course. And some of them were great, and
some of them were okay and some of them were pains
in the ass, and some of them were awful. Which is how
the world is, except that the ones who were awful
seemed really, exceptionally awful. They were loud and
belligerent and abusive and they walked down the hall in
packs and they were so loud, and I couldn't understand a
word they were saying, and they would glare at me, and
if I didn't get out of their way they ran me over. They
pushed me aside.

ROSS. The way they've been pushed aside all their lives.

SARAH. And so I tried to tell myself. Now I know how it
feels, I said. But you know what? That worked for about
a minute. And then I just got pissed off. They were so
fucking rude and loud and stupid.

ROSS. All of them?

SARAH *(beat)*. No. There were plenty of nice kids, but
they weren't the ones you noticed. You noticed the awful ones because they dominated the landscape. *(Beat.)*
And I was living in Chicago and I was taking the train to
work and it was the same thing on the train. There'd be
a dozen black people sitting quietly, going about their
business but there'd be two incredibly loud, stinky, of-

fensive black guys at one end of the car and they'd be
the ones I'd notice. And I'd tell myself not to pay attention to them. That they weren't representative of their
entire race. I knew that. I kept telling myself I just had
to get used to them. It was just a matter of learning.
(*Taking full responsibility.*) But then I noticed that I'd
started slipping into a pattern, when I got on the train.
First I'd look for an empty seat next to a white woman.
And then a white man. And then a black woman, and
then, last choice, a black man. And sometimes, if the
only empty seats were next to black men and if they
were wearing big puffy coats, then I would just stand.
(*Beat.*) And then I started adding categories. White men,
then Hispanic men, then Middle Eastern men—no Asian
men—*then* Middle Eastern men, and finally, always last,
black men. Then I started qualifying things. If the black
women had kids, then they came after some of the men,
because the kids were a pain in the ass. Their mothers
didn't watch them and they'd fall down and cry and then
their mothers would yell at them for falling down.
They'd yell, "That's what you get for standing up in the
seat." (*Beat.*) "That's what you get." (*Small beat. Matter of fact.*) I felt bad about it at first. I'd get on the train
and I'd wonder, what must that poor black man think,
I'm so obviously avoiding him. He's a perfectly nice
person. Sitting there. I see his face. He's a perfectly nice
person. But I didn't want to take a chance. And, after a
while, it sort of slipped my mind to feel bad about it.
And then everything sort of slipped my mind. So that,
when I found myself sitting across from my students and
thinking that they were scary, or that their hair was stupid, or that it was no wonder they were pregnant, I knew

it was wrong, but I didn't care. I just felt tired, contemptuous. They weren't going to listen to me. They weren't going to graduate from college. They weren't going to do anything with their lives. Not because they couldn't, but because they didn't want to. Because they were lazy and stupid.

ROSS. No they weren't. They were poor. They were high-risk students—

SARAH. I know all that, I know, I know. I knew that then. I know it now. And I never said anything... anything untoward. I was scrupulous. But I still looked at them and thought that they were worthless.

ROSS. But you were encountering them after an economic and educational system had utterly failed them.

SARAH. I know.

ROSS. So you were aware of this?

SARAH. Yes. I was fully aware. Aware of the forces that shaped me, that shaped them, and yet unable to stop thinking that if they just wanted to, they could stop being so stupid.

ROSS. So what happened? Please tell me that you... that you went to a priest and confessed and were absolved or something. Tell me something.

SARAH. No. I didn't. I just went to work and kept quiet about it. I guess I kept hoping it would go away. But then, it was like I had a viral infection that would flare up at the worst possible moments, and I started saying these... things.

ROSS. What sort of things?

SARAH. Well, this once, I was at the faculty Christmas party and I got drunk and I told this English professor how much I hate Toni Morrison.

ROSS. You hate Toni Morrison?

SARAH. Yes.

ROSS. Why?

SARAH. Her books suck.

ROSS. That is so inane.

SARAH. They do though. *Beloved* sucked. Stylistically it's a mess. It's like a sloppy first draft. Third person, first person. Realism, magical realism.

ROSS. You're imposing traditional standards for a narrative structure on it that don't allow—

SARAH. Yeah, yeah, Eurocentric, patriarchal standards and she's resisting and I'm saying rewrite. I know why I'm supposed to like her, but I don't. And I don't think that hating Toni Morrison makes you a racist. I just know that other people think it makes you a racist. *(Beat.)*

ROSS. What's your point exactly?

SARAH. My point is that I didn't need to tell that professor that I don't like Toni Morrison, but I needed to tell him something. What I really wanted to do was unburden myself completely. To get it out of my system somehow. *(Beat. ROSS regards her.)*

ROSS. So you still feel this way?

SARAH. Yes. It's just maybe not as bad, because there are hardly any black people here.

ROSS. You moved to Vermont.

SARAH. Yeah.

ROSS. You ran away.

SARAH. I didn't know what else to do. I was afraid of the kind of thoughts that popped into my head. I was afraid of what I might say. *(Small beat.)* Belmont, Vermont. Beautiful mountain, green mountain. I knew it would be quiet and clean and white. It wasn't a noble way to save myself but it was the only way I could think of. *(Beat.)* But now I'm back where I started.

ROSS. But you're not a dog.

SARAH. Of course I'm not.

ROSS. So you can help being a racist. You act like you can't, like a dog can't help chewing up the furniture, but you're not a dog, you're a human with a human-sized brain that works very well and that understands the dynamics of racism and yet here you stand, a racist. It's almost like you're proud of it.

SARAH. I'm not proud. I'm at a loss. I say to myself over and over and over again, "Just stop it! You know you're doing it, just stop it!" and I still do it anyway. And it doesn't help that when I try and articulate what's going on in my head, in even the mildest way, I'm attacked.

ROSS. What do you want people to do? Congratulate you?

SARAH. No. But couldn't they listen to me? Or talk to me? Couldn't they admit, that on occasion even, they feel the same way?

ROSS. So you're suggesting what?

SARAH *(shrugs)*. Stop being stupid. Admit defeat.

ROSS. Don't back away. You're suggesting a real dialogue.

SARAH. Ideally, sure, but it's impossible.

ROSS. That's not true.

SARAH. Public dialogue is never real dialogue. Nobody will admit to anything in a crowd. I mean, I can't believe I'm the only person who feels this way.

ROSS. All right. I'll admit something. I've never been able to look at an African American without noting that he or she is such.

SARAH. You mean, when you look at a black person you think, "There's a black person."

ROSS. Yes.

SARAH. Oooh. That's ugly.

ROSS. Well—

SARAH. That's pathetic! That's the most you can admit?

ROSS. All right! Let's say I'm secretly the grand hooba of the KKK. Okay? Now what? Where do we go from here?

SARAH (hesitates). I don't know.

ROSS. Well you can't just criticize and criticize and never offer a solution.

SARAH. If I had a solution I'd put it in a goddamned bulleted list! (Beat.)

ROSS. You're a terrible coward. Even if you can't find the perfect solution, you should find the best you can and at least give it a try.

SARAH. You mean, like, have a forum?

ROSS. Okay, it was a bad idea, but at least I tried. You have to go out on a limb. Otherwise the best lack all conviction.

SARAH. What?

ROSS. Yeats. "The best lack all conviction while the worst are full of passionate intensity."

SARAH. The best lack all conviction.

ROSS. The worst are full of passionate intensity.

SARAH (beat). And I'm which?

ROSS. Neither right now, you're just awful. (Pause.) Look, I'm sorry. I mean, obviously you've struggled with this. You're struggling with this now, I can tell. But I don't think that just because you've struggled, you should be let off the hook. I think Catherine's right. I think you should come up with a plan.

SARAH. I don't know.

ROSS. You've got ideas already.

SARAH. I don't have anything.

ROSS. What about that recruiting program you were telling me about? The thing you did at Lancaster. That was a nice idea.

SARAH. It didn't work.

ROSS. It completely failed?

SARAH. Well, there was about a forty-percent success rate.

ROSS. In fact, it did quite well. See, Sarah, for all your professed resignation, I think that inherent in what you're saying, is hope.

SARAH. What do you mean?

ROSS. Most people are just racists. They don't know they're racists. *(Beat.)* I know you have some good ideas.

SARAH. God.

ROSS. Don't put up barriers to this. I trust you. I trust you can do this.

SARAH. Why?

ROSS. I just do. *(Beat.)*

SARAH. Why don't you leave me alone?

ROSS. Are you going to try?

SARAH *(beat)*. Yeah. Just leave me alone. *(ROSS starts to go.)* Hey. Thanks for being so nice to me.

ROSS. I wasn't being nice. *(Beat. This is very hard for him.)* That thing, with the train? Choosing the seats? I do that too.

SARAH. Everybody does.

ROSS. That doesn't make it right.

SARAH. I know. *(Beat. Frustrated.)* I know, I know, I know.

BLACKOUT

SCENE FOUR

Sarah's office, the following morning. She has fallen asleep at her desk. MR. MEYERS enters, holding a piece of paper.

MEYERS. Sarah?

SARAH. What?! ... Oh God. I fell asleep.

MEYERS. I thought you should see this. *(Hands her the paper. She reads.)*

SARAH. Oh God.

MEYERS. Do you want me to go with you?

SARAH. I ... maybe I should go by myself.

MEYERS. Whatever you think's best. I'll walk you as far as my office.

SARAH. Thanks.

(They exit, closing the door behind them.

The chapel bells begin to chime their quarter-hour tune. The door opens again and KENNEY enters. She looks around then goes to Sarah's desk and picks up the phone and dials.)

KENNEY. President Garvey, please, Marion. *(Beat. She begins looking through SARAH's papers as she waits.)* He isn't? Are you sure? *(Beat.)* Fine. *(She hangs up. She is holding the legal pad. She reads. There are several used pages folded over the back of the pad and she flips them over and reads from the beginning. She doesn't look pleased. She takes the legal pad and leaves.)*

BLACKOUT

SCENE FIVE

Sarah's office a couple of hours later. GREG SULLIVAN is waiting for her. SARAH enters quickly. She isn't happy to see him.

GREG. Hi, Dean Daniels! They said I could wait.

SARAH. Yes?

GREG. Greg Sullivan? Students for Tolerance?

SARAH. And?

GREG. I wondered, could we talk?

SARAH. Actually no, we can't. I'm in the middle of something.

GREG. Oh I'm sorry. Should I make an appointment?

SARAH. There's an idea. *(She perfunctorily picks up her appointment book.)* Tomorrow at one?

GREG. Terrific. Thanks so much.

(He leaves. SARAH closes the door behind him then goes to her desk and picks up the phone. Right away, though, she sees that the legal pad is missing. She hangs up the phone and starts looking for it.)

SARAH. Shit. *(She picks up the phone again and dials. Into phone.)* Did you come take my list? *(Beat.)* I need to talk to you. ... Ross, please. ... Okay. Thanks. *(She hangs up.)*

(There's a knock on the door. SARAH looks around, then ducks underneath her desk, hiding. The door opens and KENNEY sticks her head in.)

KENNEY. Sarah?

(She hurries toward the desk and without seeing SARAH, quickly puts the legal pad back where it was, trying to make it look as if nothing has been disturbed. She quickly leaves. SARAH cautiously emerges, studies the legal pad. A knock on the door. SARAH ducks back under the desk. The door opens and ROSS enters.)

ROSS. Sarah?

(SARAH emerges again, banging her head.)

SARAH. Ow.

ROSS. What are you doing?

SARAH. Picking up a...hiding. Close the door. *(He does.)* She had it.

ROSS. Who?

SARAH. Catherine. She came in here and took it and then she brought it back and left it here for me. It's a trap.

ROSS. What?

SARAH. My list. I'm going to get fired.

ROSS. Let me see. *(She hands him the pad.)* These are good suggestions. I've always wanted a cultural studies program—

SARAH. Not that crap! Look back! Before that.

ROSS *(flips back a few pages, reads)*. Sarah. You didn't get rid of this? *(Sees something.)* What is this?

SARAH. The pros and cons of living near black people versus living away from them.

ROSS *(reads)*. "Away: not scary. You forget about their hair." What were you doing?

SARAH. I just...you know, I had to get it all out.

ROSS. Why did you ever leave this where somebody could find it?

SARAH. I had to go. I had to go talk to Simon. Ross. He
was doing it to himself.

ROSS. What?

SARAH. He ... the FBI, they sent us the results. *(She pulls a
folded piece of paper out of her pocket.)* The handwriting was his. He was doing it to himself. *(ROSS stares at
her.)* I went to his room, and I asked him. I said, "Simon? Did you do this?" And he just nodded and sat
down on his bed and he started crying. *(Small beat.)* Finally, he said it was like somebody else was doing it. He
said that he can remember watching his hand as he
wrote. He can see his hands folding the paper. He can
see his hands taping it to his door. He said he knew he'd
get caught but he did it anyway.

ROSS. He can't explain it?

SARAH. I didn't think I should ... I didn't ask him to. He
just said he was relieved it was finally over.

ROSS. The poor kid. All this time, he's just been waiting.

SARAH. He said he was sorry. *(Pause.)* I don't know what
to do, Ross.

ROSS. About what?

SARAH. I kept looking at his hands. When Simon said that. I
kept looking at his hands. We were sitting there on his
bed and he was crying and we were both staring at his
hands and there they were. Hands. Just hands. Next to
each other. Mine in my lap. His in his. I looked at his
hands and then I looked at mine. At my fingers. The
backs of my hands. I just kept thinking, "This is me.
This is me. This is me." *(Beat.)* And I looked at Simon,
and I thought, "That's you." I rubbed the back of his
hand and I thought, "That's you. And you're crying."
(Disgusted with herself.) And I don't know what to say.

ROSS. It's okay.

SARAH. No it's not.

ROSS (*not going to her*). Of course it's not. I just...I don't know. I can't tell you what to do, Sarah.

BLACKOUT

SCENE SIX

Sarah's office, a couple of hours later. KENNEY, STRAUSS, ROSS, MR. MEYERS and SARAH are there. MEYERS sits quietly in a corner.

KENNEY. Well this changes everything.

ROSS. What does it change, exactly?

KENNEY. Everything. This is quite a development. (*Laughs.*) He's clearly quite a study, isn't he? What was he thinking?

SARAH. He doesn't know.

STRAUSS. It's a textbook case. Internalized racism. Is he dark skinned?

SARAH. Compared to what?

STRAUSS. Light-skinned blacks. It's an issue, apparently, either way. Jean Toomer, for example—

SARAH. Jean Toomer?

STRAUSS. One of the foremost writers of the Harlem Renaissance.

SARAH. I know who Jean Toomer is.

STRAUSS. Oh.

SARAH. What does he have to do with Simon?

STRAUSS. I was just trying to make a point.

SARAH. You don't know Simon.

STRAUSS. Well, I—

SARAH. I don't think you've ever spoken to him.

STRAUSS. No.

SARAH. So you don't know him.

STRAUSS. Yes I do. *(Beat.)* He's Little Black Sambo.

ROSS. What?!

STRAUSS. Isn't that how he referred to himself in the notes?

ROSS. Yes.

STRAUSS. And what did Little Black Sambo do?

KENNEY. Just tell us.

STRAUSS. Well Little Black Sambo had some beautiful new clothes and he was walking in the jungle, showing them off, when a tiger jumped out of the bush and threatened to eat him. So Little Black Sambo offered the tiger his new coat in exchange for his life and the tiger agreed and took his coat. And then another tiger popped up and so on and so on until the tigers had taken all of his clothes. Little Black Sambo was going home naked and forlorn when he heard a terrible noise coming from the forest and he peeped around a tree and saw all of the tigers wearing his clothes and arguing over which of them was the grandest tiger of all. They argued and argued until they got so angry that they took off the clothes and started chasing each other around a tree. Well Little Black Sambo saw this and he walked up and calmly put his clothes back on, knowing that the tigers were too intent on each other to pay him any mind. The tigers just kept chasing each other, faster and faster around the tree. They began spinning and spinning until they were just a yellow blur and they spun so fast, they spun themselves into butter. So Little Black Sambo got himself a spoon and scooped up the butter and put it on his pancakes and ate the tigers up. *(He laughs.)* Which is just what Simon Brick did to us. He pulled one over on us. Got us all in whirl over nothing.

SARAH. It doesn't have anything to do with us.

ROSS. And it wasn't nothing.

STRAUSS. He's a little fox. A little con man.

SARAH. Think of him.

STRAUSS. He's probably bragging about it to his friends right now.

SARAH. Imagine him for half a second. That is not why he did it.

STRAUSS. Why then?

SARAH. I don't know.

STRAUSS. You don't know? But you're so in touch with him.

SARAH. I never claimed to be "in touch" with anybody.

STRAUSS. Don't be so modest. Tell us about the black man. Illuminate us. *(Pause.)*

SARAH *(to KENNEY)*. You showed it to him, didn't you? You came in here and took it, and then you showed it to him.

KENNEY *(beat. Considers)*. It was in plain view. Lying on your desk.

SARAH. You had no right to read it.

KENNEY. It was in plain view. *(Beat.)* Would you like to explain?

SARAH. No.

ROSS. You know, you've seen something out of context and—

KENNEY. You know about this?

ROSS. If you'll let me finish, I think that to judge Sarah by
what you've seen is unfair.

KENNEY. I'm asking her to explain it to me, right now.
She says there's no explanation.

STRAUSS. Except the obvious one which is that she's a
racist.

SARAH. There is an explanation but I choose not to tell it
to you.

ROSS. Sarah has been doing some soul searching—

SARAH. I choose not to tell it to them! *(To STRAUSS and
KENNEY, picking up the pad.)* Just use what you know.
Public transportation? Scary! Toni Morrison? I hate her!
So what if she won the Nobel Prize? So did Pearl S.
Buck! La la la. *(They stare at her.)* Satisfied?

KENNEY. That really wasn't what I was looking for.

STRAUSS. Really. That was weird.

SARAH *(reaching in her drawer, handing KENNEY an envelope).* Here. Let's get this over with.

KENNEY. What's this?

SARAH. My letter of resignation.

ROSS. When did you do that?

SARAH. Just before the meeting.

KENNEY *(looking at the letter).* Fine. I'll pass it on to
President Garvey.

ROSS *(to SARAH).* Don't you want to talk about it first?

KENNEY. There's nothing to talk about. If she hadn't
given it to me I would have asked for it. Now, about
Simon—I'll have to call his parents, but I think we'll
want him off campus as soon as possible. Mr. Meyers?
Why don't you go over and tell him that he's been asked
to leave and help him pack his things. Then you can
drive him home.

MEYERS. Ma'am?

SARAH (overlapping). Wait a minute. Drive him home? Aren't you going to talk to him first?

KENNEY. Simon wrote the notes, which means he's been lying to us all along, which means he's violated the honor code. That's grounds for expulsion. And fraud.

SARAH. But he feels terrible. Give him a chance to explain if he wants to.

KENNEY. The quickest way to heal is to get on with things. Mr. Meyers? Go tell him.

MEYERS. No ma'am.

KENNEY. What?

MEYERS. I'm not telling him that. I'll help him out with his things, but I won't be the bearer of bad news.

STRAUSS. Let me tell him.

SARAH. No!

STRAUSS. I want to meet him.

SARAH. I'll do it.

KENNEY. You've quit.

SARAH. I don't want you near him!

STRAUSS. How do we know you won't go in there and scream "I hate Toni Morrison!" at him?

SARAH. I have always been polite.

STRAUSS. You haven't been polite to me.

SARAH. That's because I hate you. You so totally suck.

ROSS (overlapping). Let's not do this. Sarah?

SARAH. There, that's out in the open. Okay?

STRAUSS. It was hardly a secret.

SARAH. You hate me too, okay?

STRAUSS. Whatever you say, dear.

SARAH. I'm going to talk to Simon, though, and you're not going near him. Me! Not you.

KENNEY. You're all riled up.

SARAH. I'll be fine. I promise. *(She exits.)*

KENNEY *(going after her)*. Sarah—

ROSS *(stops her)*. I'll go with her.

MEYERS. Me too.

KENNEY *(considers for half a second)*. Oh fine. All three of you go. But Ross, I'm holding you responsible.
(ROSS exits, followed by MEYERS.)

STRAUSS. I can't believe you let her go.

KENNEY. Well, she hasn't actually done anything overt. She was doing a good job until all of this came up.

STRAUSS. It doesn't bother me if she hates me. I mean, she's obviously insane.

KENNEY. You know, maybe I'll wait and let Simon's parents call me.

STRAUSS. What?

KENNEY. Simon's parents. I think I'll wait and let them call me. That way he'll be home and they won't try to come up here and talk things out.

STRAUSS. Whatever you think is best.

KENNEY. I feel sorry for Simon. I'm afraid it will take him some time to recover from this.

STRAUSS. He'll be fine.

KENNEY. I think he just wanted attention.

STRAUSS. No. He's a little con artist. *(Smiles.)* A crafty little fox.

BLACKOUT

SCENE SEVEN

Sarah's office, the next day. She is packing up boxes.
ROSS is talking to her.

ROSS. I understand completely why you quit. But I still
wish there were some other way.

SARAH. There's not.

ROSS. I just think that you've changed. I think this thing
with Simon forced you to see yourself in a different
way. You had an epiphany.

SARAH. No, because I don't believe in shit like that. Ergo
my previous, completely fraudulent "awakening." It
didn't take. Because there are no transformational moments. You don't become a better person overnight.

ROSS. Then yesterday was a turning point.

SARAH. No.

ROSS. Well would you be open to the possibility, that
maybe someday, it might be conceivable, that you could,
perhaps, change?

SARAH. No.

ROSS. Well I don't believe you. Look, I have to go, I have
a class. Can you meet me for a beer later? I still want to
talk about this.

SARAH. No.

ROSS. Six o clock?

SARAH. I said no.

ROSS. Should I come by here?

SARAH. Come by if you want, I won't be here.

ROSS. Yes you will. *(He takes the Rilke from the shelf*
where she's put it, and puts it in her box . Exits.)

SARAH *(yelling after him)*. Know-it-all!

(MR. MEYERS enters and knocks on her open door.)

SARAH. Hi.

MEYERS. Hi.

SARAH. How'd it go?

MEYERS. Okay.

SARAH. He's home?

MEYERS. Safe and sound.

SARAH. So. I'm leaving.

MEYERS. I see that. *(Pause.)*

SARAH. What'd you talk about? On the way?

MEYERS. Not a lot. Baseball. He thinks the Pirates might
    have a chance at something in a couple of years. They're
    a young team. They still have something to prove.

SARAH. That's nice.

MEYERS. Yeah.

SARAH. Were his parents home?

MEYERS. No. He let himself in. I helped him carry his
    things. He offered me a Diet Coke. I didn't really want
    one but I did ask to use the restroom.

SARAH. What was the house like?

MEYERS. Nothing special. Not too big, not too little. The
    bathroom was nice. I guess it was a guest bathroom.
    They had the liquid soap in the dispenser, though, so
    you could really wash your hands. Sometimes, people
    put little special soaps in the guest bathroom. Little
    soaps shaped like roses or something. I never know if
    I'm supposed to use them or just look at them.

SARAH *(beat)*. Did he seem sad?

MEYERS. Not really. We stopped at a Burger King. I hope
    that's okay. I bought him dinner.

SARAH. That's fine.

MEYERS. He has a hearty appetite.

SARAH. Did he say anything?

MEYERS. I didn't ask.

SARAH. So he never...

MEYERS. He did say that he maybe made a mistake, asking for his own room. He said it left him feeling kind of lonely.

SARAH. He said that?

MEYERS. He said he's shy to start with, so maybe he shouldn't of cut himself off from people like that.

SARAH. He said he's shy?

MEYERS. That's how he put it.

SARAH. Anything else?

MEYERS. Nope. Mostly we didn't say anything. I asked him, did he want me to stay until his parents got home. He said, nothing personal, but he kind of felt like he was under arrest, so would I mind leaving? I said, "Not at all." *(Beat.)* When I got home last night, I woke my wife up and I told her what all had happened, and she said it seemed like a shame, such a nice kid like that, doing himself in. So to speak.

SARAH. It is a shame.

MEYERS. So where you headed?

SARAH. I'm going back to Chicago.

MEYERS. Can you get your old job back?

SARAH. I don't think so.

MEYERS. Does this kind of look bad for you then?

SARAH. It kind of does. But I don't know. I don't think I'm suited to this line of work.

MEYERS. Maybe not. *(Beat.)*

SARAH. Well, thanks for all your help.

MEYERS. Yeah. I just wish it could of turned out different.

SARAH. Me too.

MEYERS. No. I guess, I mean, I wish *you* could of turned out different.

SARAH. Pardon?

MEYERS. I thought, when we started this, that you weren't like them. You didn't want to make speeches or stand up in front of everybody, you just wanted to get down to work. I thought you were different. But I guess you were just hiding out, huh?

SARAH. I'm not sure I understand.

MEYERS. Well, I don't usually trade in rumors, but people are saying that you ... said some things.

SARAH. I see.

MEYERS. So, is what they're saying true?

SARAH. Yes. It's true.

MEYERS. Then, I guess that upsets me. You know? I guess I looked at Simon last night, and I figured that he wouldn't of done that to himself if somebody hadn't made him feel bad. If somebody hadn't put the words in his head. You know? I mean, those notes, they were mean and terrible, and I don't think you see yourself like that, like he did in those notes, if somebody hasn't already seen you that way first. That's all.

SARAH. I ... yes. *(Beat.)* I'm sorry if I disappointed you.

MEYERS. I guess I just liked that kid.

SARAH. I like Simon too.

MEYERS. Then how can you think those things?

SARAH. I guess that's what I have to figure out.

MEYERS. That seems kind of easy.

SARAH. It does?

MEYERS. Yeah. I mean, one part of you must be lying to the other part.

SARAH. What?

MEYERS. Either you're not as good as you think you are, or you're not as bad as you think you are.

SARAH. I really do like Simon.

MEYERS. That's promising.

SARAH. But the other part of me is not lying. *(Pause.)*

MEYERS. Well, I hope you figure it out.

SARAH. Me too.

(GREG enters.)

GREG. Hi.

SARAH. Yes?

GREG. I had an appointment? *(SARAH laughs.)* Is this a bad time?

SARAH. Yes, I've sort of ...

MEYERS. She quit.

GREG. Oh. My. I'm sorry. Or, congratulations, maybe, I don't know.

SARAH. Let's go with congratulations.

GREG. Okay then. Congratulations.

SARAH. Thanks.

GREG. I wanted to see you about Students for Tolerance. We have a problem.

SARAH. Well you'll have to ask Dean Strauss to help you.

GREG. Dean Strauss is the problem.

SARAH. Oh.

GREG. I really don't know who else to talk to.

MEYERS. I'll leave you two alone.

SARAH. Wait. *(She offers her hand.)* Thanks for everything.

MEYERS *(shakes her hand).* Good luck to you then, Sarah.
(He exits, closing the door behind him.)

SARAH. So what is it?

GREG. Well, Dean Strauss wanted to come to the meetings, which was fine, at first, but then, he wouldn't shut
up. And the whole point of the group was to have a
place where the students could talk, one on one.

SARAH. I thought the whole point was to get you into law
school. *(Beat. GREG is taken aback, but then he laughs.)*

GREG. Okay. That's fair. That's fair. I can see how you
would think that. But you know, I've always been taught
that you should capitalize on your strengths, and that's
all I was trying to do. Was to kill two birds with one
stone. So to speak.

SARAH. I see.

GREG. But I'm seriously committed to this group now. And
we need somebody's help. I mean, I didn't know how
good the group could be until I lied to Dean Strauss—

SARAH. You lied to him?

GREG. Just to get rid of him for a while. I told him we had to
cancel the next couple of meetings because of mid-terms,
but then we had a secret meeting in my room. It was
kind of silly, but it went so much better without him
there. We really started to talk about our experiences with
African Americans, or, to be more precise, our complete
lack of experience which was only compounded by the
fact that there were still no black students in the group.

SARAH. Aha.

GREG. Right. It was ridiculous. So I got an idea. When I
heard that the Black Student Union was boycotting the
forums, I gave Claudia Thompson a call. You know,
their president?

SARAH. Yes, I know Claudia.

GREG. And I said, "Look, we've got this little group going, it's not much, but we're committed to opening up a real dialogue about race. The only problem is, we're all white."

SARAH. What did she say to that?

GREG. She laughed. So I asked her if the BSU would join us at our next meeting. And when I told her that we were meeting in my room, you know, so we could avoid Dean Strauss, that convinced her we were okay. So she offered the Union house and we met there last night.

SARAH. You did?

GREG. And it was terrific. It was awkward at first but then we really got into it and people were saying things... things I'd never expect anybody to admit to. But it was all so open. You know? The spirit was right.

SARAH. The spirit?

GREG. Yes. The spirit was right. And so we all just opened up. And afterwards we had a huge group hug and we're meeting again next week.

SARAH. Really?

GREG. Yeah.

SARAH. How many people? In this group hug?

GREG. I'd say fifteen, total.

SARAH (*smiles*). *You* were in a group hug.

GREG. Yes. I know it probably seems stupid to you...

SARAH. No. Not stupid. Just, I guess I'm a little surprised.

GREG. Yeah. Me too I guess.

SARAH. Huh. (*Small beat.*) So what can I do for you, Greg?

GREG. Well we can't have Dean Strauss come back. It would ruin everything.

SARAH. Would you like me to find you another sponsor?

GREG. Do we have to have a sponsor at all?

SARAH *(considers)*. No. In fact, I think it'd be better if
   you didn't.

GREG. That's kind of what we thought, too.

SARAH. Let me take care of it for you.

GREG. Thank you so much. *(He shakes her hand.)*

SARAH. It will be my last official duty.

GREG. I was wondering, before I go, could I ask you
   something about Simon Brick?

SARAH. Yes?

GREG. We heard that he did this to himself.

SARAH. He did.

GREG. Do you know why?

SARAH. I don't.

GREG. Huh. You know, we talked about this a lot last
   night. About Simon. Why would he do it.

SARAH. And what did you conclude?

GREG. We didn't conclude anything. All we could do was
   guess. Simon wasn't there.

SARAH. Right.

GREG. In fact, we kept asking all the black people there,
   you know, why did he do it? And finally, this guy Jason
   said, "I don't know why he did it. It's not like we all
   think alike, just because we're black." You know? His
   whole point was that he wasn't the spokesperson for his
   race. He said, "That's just one of those things you white
   people assume about blacks. That we all think alike."
   But then, this girl Lisa said, "But, now you're saying
   that all *white* people think alike. How is that any different?" *(Laughs.)* We went around and around with that
   for an hour practically.

SARAH. It's hard, isn't it?

GREG. Yeah, it's hard. But I think it's important to try.

SARAH. To go out on a limb.

GREG. Exactly.

SARAH *(nods. Beat)*. All right, Greg. Good luck with the group.

GREG. Thanks a lot. Seriously. And good luck to you, too.

SARAH. Thank you. *(He leaves. SARAH turns and walks to her windows. She looks outside. The morning light is very bright. For a moment, she watches the campus. The chapel bells chime. It is one o'clock. She turns and goes to her phone. She picks up a file and opens it, checks a number, and dials. On phone.)* Simon? ... Hi. It's Sarah Daniels. *(Small beat.)* Right. Dean Daniels. I just wanted to call and see how things went with your parents last night. Mr. Meyers said they weren't home yet, when you got there. *(Beat.)* So were they mad? *(Small beat.)* Oh God. Dean Kenney was supposed to call them. So they just came in and there you were? What'd you do? *(Laughs.)* Well, at least you have a sense of humor about it. That's a good sign, I think. ... Right. *(Beat. Slowly.)* Simon, here's why I really called. I don't know how to start this, even ... it's no big deal, I guess, I just ... I haven't asked you this, because I wanted to respect your feelings, and I didn't want to pry. Or that's what I was telling myself. But now I'm wondering if I didn't ask because I was afraid. That it might be awkward. Or that I might ... stumble. But I was just wondering ... do you want to talk about it? *(Beat. She listens, still for a moment, then begins to nod as he speaks.)*

LIGHTS FADE
END OF PLAY

DIRECTOR'S NOTES

DIRECTOR'S NOTES

DIRECTOR'S NOTES

DIRECTOR'S NOTES

DIRECTOR'S NOTES

DIRECTOR'S NOTES